Ordnance Survey
South Devon
and Dartmoor
Landranger Guidebook

D0769978

How to use this Guide

Pre-planning:
First look at the KEY MAP section — this shows the area covered, the towns and villages, and the starting point for the 12 Walks and 10 Tours. If you are unfamiliar with the area, look up some of the towns and villages in the PLACES OF INTEREST section. The WALKS or TOURS will provide further local information. The introductions will give you a feeling for the history, landscape, and wildlife of the area.

On the Spot:
From your chosen base, explore the area by road or on foot. Stars (★) after a place name indicate that it is featured in the PLACES OF INTEREST section (this is necessary as it is not possible to include every village and town because of space limitations). Some 28 places of interest are accompanied by maps to enable you to plan a short stroll. The scale of these is 2½ INCHES to 1 MILE (see CONVENTIONAL SIGNS for rights of way etc).

Landranger Maps:
These are the natural companions to the Guide. Places of interest are identified first with the number of the Landranger Map on which it appears (sometimes more than one). This is followed by two letters indicating the National Grid Square and by a 4-figure reference number. To locate any place or feature referred to on the relevant Landranger map, first read the two figures along the north or south edges of the map, then the two figures along the east or west edges. Trace the lines adjacent to each of the two sets of figures across the map face, and the point where they intersect will be the south-west corner of the grid square in which the place or feature lies.

Acknowledgements

We should like to thank those individuals and organisations who helped in the compilation of this book: Neil Curtis who, with support from Sheila Dallas and Richard Garratt, chose the walks and tours, suggested the photographic selection, and compiled and wrote the majority of the text; Sarah Loweth, and especially Paul Gompertz of Devon Wildlife Trust for contributing 'Natural History of South Devon and Dartmoor'; David Walker of East Devon Group Ramblers' Association for help with the route of Walk 2; Neil Devons of Torbay Tourist Board; Gillian Taylor and John Weir of Dartmoor National Park Office; Eric Wallis of The South West Way Association; Su Powell of South Hams District Council; Lynne Dunn of Teignbridge District Council; Borough of West Devon Office Services; Sandra Collins and Sue Challacombe of Devon Tourism; Anthony Adam, Devon Regional Office of the National Trust and the National Trust staff at Lydford Gorge; Nigel Buckler of West Country Tourist Board; Margaret Davy of the Dartmoor Preservation Association; the staff of Becky Falls Estate; Paula Chasty for the artwork; Curtis Garratt Limited for editing, designing, and typesetting the guide.

Contents

KEY MAP INDEX

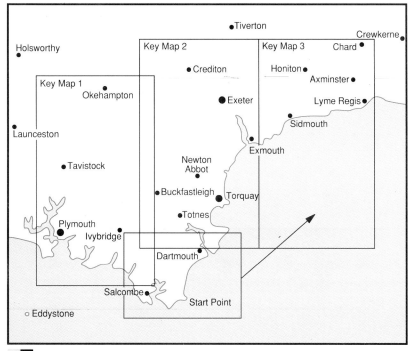

- Tiverton
- Crewkerne
- Holsworthy
- Key Map 2
- Chard
- Key Map 3
- Honiton
- Crediton
- Axminster
- Key Map 1
- Okehampton
- Exeter
- Lyme Regis
- Launceston
- Sidmouth
- Exmouth
- Tavistock
- Newton Abbot
- Buckfastleigh
- Torquay
- Totnes
- Plymouth
- Ivybridge
- Dartmouth
- Salcombe
- Start Point
- Eddystone

Symbol	Description
4	Motor and Cycle Tour Start
6	Walk Start
	Mini-Walk Start

LANDRANGER MAPS OF SOUTH DEVON AND DARTMOOR

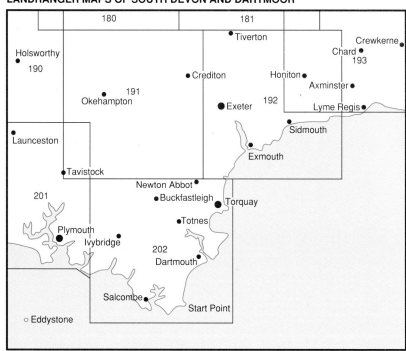

- 180
- 181
- Tiverton
- Crewkerne
- Holsworthy
- Chard
- 190
- 193
- Crediton
- Honiton
- 191
- Axminster
- Okehampton
- Exeter
- 192
- Lyme Regis
- Launceston
- Sidmouth
- Exmouth
- Tavistock
- Newton Abbot
- 201
- Buckfastleigh
- Torquay
- Totnes
- Plymouth
- Ivybridge
- 202
- Dartmouth
- Salcombe
- Start Point
- Eddystone

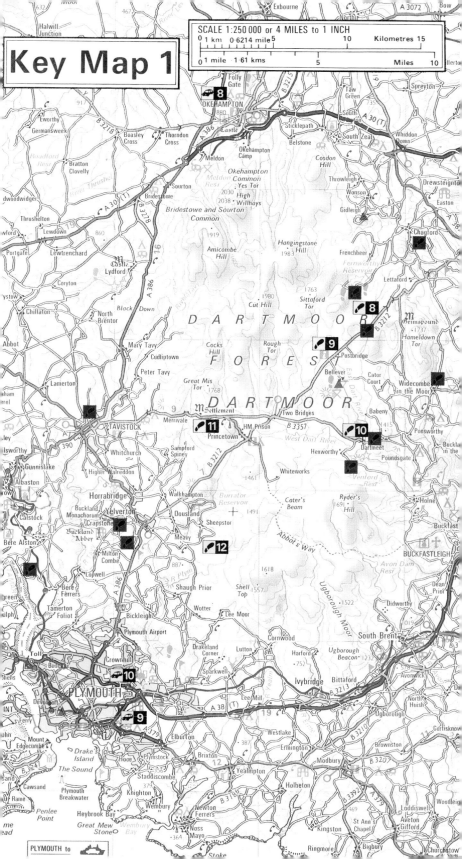

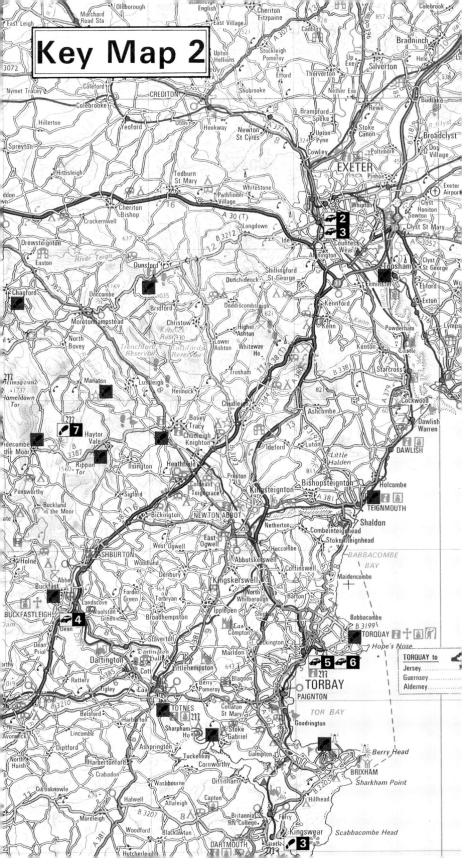

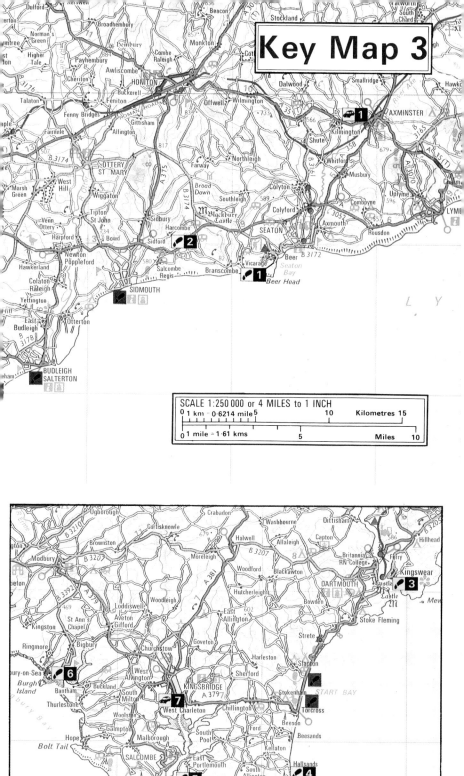

Key Map 3

SCALE 1:250 000 or 4 MILES to 1 INCH

0 1 km = 0·6214 mile 5   10   Kilometres 15

0 1 mile = 1·61 kms   5   Miles   10

Introduction
South Devon and
Dartmoor

At least one Arthurian legend has it that the noble and chivalrous king was born at Tintagel in Cornwall and held court, with his knights seated around the famous Round Table, at a castle on the site of Cadbury Hill in Somerset. It seems odd, somehow, that such a great fifth-century ruler would deliberately ignore Devon, especially when the countryside described in so many of the tales of the gallant knights seems exactly to fit what we can see of the county today.

Though perhaps not dating back to King Arthur's time, there are castles aplenty in South Devon, and one could easily imagine evil black knights astride great chargers barring the way to travellers wishing to cross the county's clapper bridges although, once again, these post-date the Round Table days. There are clear, sparkling waters where a shimmering, ethereal hand might have held the mighty Excalibur aloft. Woodlands and forest abound where fire-breathing dragons or evil witches would have lurked to plot the downfall of Sir Lancelot or Galahad. Perhaps the cunning wizard Merlin concocted his spells hidden deep among the oaks of a once more extensive Wistman's Wood. Where better could stout and pure men of brave deeds and words have searched for the elusive Holy Grail than on the barren heights of Dartmoor which, even by the fifth century, would have seemed a land rich in mystery and legend? It is known that Crusaders set out from South Devon's coast to gain glory in the Holy Land, but did fragile boats leave the rocky shores more than half a millennium earlier with passengers intent on vanquishing foreign foes? And, if you stroll down one of South Devon's narrow, sunken lanes aglow with wild flowers, you can almost hear the clatter of horse's hoofs and the clinking of armour.

The stories do not seem to attribute such honourable men or valiant goings on to Devon, however — perhaps it is that the county has more than enough to offer today's travellers, and has no need to lay claim to hosting Arthur's court. In former times, a journey from the country's capital to the wild moors, lush pasture land, quiet hamlets, and rugged coasts of Devon would have seemed a long, arduous, and possibly dangerous undertaking. Today, using the M4 and M5 motorways, it is possible, traffic hold-ups permitting, to set out from London and reach Devon's

The gnarled trees with lichen- and moss-clad branches of Wistman's Wood.

Building Stone

Dartmoor granite has been used as a building stone since the Bronze Age or earlier. As the ravages of the weather causes the exposed tors to split and shatter, gravity takes the broken blocks down slope, and there has long been an abundance of naturally hewn blocks, known as moorstone, among the clitter. Bronze Age peoples built their round huts — such as those at Grimspound — by erecting a circular wall of moorstone some 3-4 feet high, with a gap for a doorway, and then raising a tent-like, timber-framed structure on top, finally made weather-proof by a layer of turf.

Later, when more sophisticated building techniques demanded better-shaped stone, granite was split into blocks by a very laborious process known as the 'wedge and groove' method. Using a hammer and wedge, a groove was cut along the length of the block of granite and gradually made deeper and deeper until, after many back-breaking hours, the block split naturally.

This method of cutting granite continued to be used right up until the beginning of the nineteenth century when it was replaced by a slightly less arduous method known as 'feather and tare'. It still involved two strong men and a good deal of labour, however. One man held a long steel chisel while the other hammered it into the rock to a depth of some 3 inches. In this way a series of holes was created along a straight line. Then, steel wedges called tares, and flanked on either side by slivers of metal called feathers, were hammered into the rock which eventually split along the line of the series of holes. Today, of course, explosives and machine tools have taken away a good deal of the hard work.

Dartmoor granite has been used for local building work, millstones, and clapper bridges but it has also found its way out of the county — for example, to construct London Bridge — and was popular towards the end of the Victorian era for the construction of granite-cobbled roads. It was for exporting granite out of Devon via the Stover Canal that Haytor Granite Tramway was constructed.

---

capital, Exeter, in three hours or less without breaking the speed limit. The South Devon and Dartmoor area, including the section east of Exeter which might be described as East Devon, is perhaps the perfect English holiday region, although some may be deterred by the throngs who speed westwards or southwards, by road or by rail, during the high season in search of good food, sunny beaches, and relaxation.

The usually dry statistics provide us with ample evidence of South Devon's popularity with holiday makers. In the mid-1980s, more than 500 million tourist nights were spent in Britain and, of these, about a fifth found their way into the West Country as a whole. But it is the Torbay area which is the most popular destination with visitors, such that some 10 million tourist nights were spent in the three resorts of Torquay, Paignton, and Brixham alone. And if we take a look at some of the climatic figures only, it is not hard to find one good reason why the area is so perennially popular — the weather. In 1984, for example, Exmouth enjoyed over a hundred days with no rain, an average temperature for the year of 65.8 °F, and more than 1000 hours of sunshine! So the notion of sitting in a country garden, bathed in sunshine and surrounded by some of Britain's most beautiful scenery, enjoying a cream tea is no fanciful one.

From the charming, and authentic fishing village of Beer in the east, across the coast of the 'English Riviera', to the busy, modern city and port of Plymouth on the east bank of the Tamar, South Devon's coast has something to offer almost everyone. And inland, there are the quiet villages and lovely rolling farmland of the South Hams, or the remote, rocky tors of Dartmoor so often described as the south of England's last truly wild place.

As well as the soft West Country maritime climate, it is the geology of the region which has shaped the county's past, present, and, no doubt, its future. Overall, the structure and composition of the rocks, which are the foundations of the land and thereby its inhabitants, are complex with a history going back more than 600 million years. The oldest rocks, Precambrian in age, are thought to be the mica- and garnet-rich gneisses which make up the so-called Eddystone Reef on which a lighthouse still stands some 14 miles out into the English Channel to the south of Plymouth.

Geologists have classified the last 560 million years or so into different periods characterized by the types of rocks and fossils found within them. One of these periods, between about 400 and 350 million years ago, has taken the name of the county where examples of its rocks are well described — this is the Devonian Period. The Devonian was a time of great activity in the Earth's history when much of the west country peninsula was, at various times, submerged beneath the sea, and when the sediments worn from the rising land to the north and south were being deposited in great thicknesses on the ocean floor. In the early part of the Devonian, however, the South Devon area was firstly a coastal plain and was later submerged by a shelf sea. The geology of South Devon is hardly so simple as this would seem to imply, however, for the beds of rocks have subsequently been thrust and sheared, overturned and folded into myriad complex arrangements.

Looking at the southern stretch of the county, from Dartmouth in the east to the Tamar, the greenish-coloured, muddy rocks of Lower Devonian age are known as the Dartmouth Slates. Fossils are not common in these rocks although some specimens of Devonian fishes have been found. At Start Point, however, you can find greenish, platy rocks glistening with crystals of mica. They occur, together with some dolomitized limestones, in a narrow band from Start Point through Salcombe, to Bolt Tail. The age of these rocks is not known for certain; they have certainly been metamorphosed by the heat and stress generated by major Earth movements but they may be of a Devonian or earlier date. Lying above the Dartmouth Slates and, therefore, of a younger age is a group of grey shales and limestones, known as the Meadsfoot Beds; they include a reasonable variety of marine and brackish-water fossil species such as the little lampshells or brachiopods and corals.

To the north of the Dartmouth Slates and Meadsfoot Beds, the Middle Devonian

Dartmoor Ponies

Visitors to Dartmoor expect to see the moorland ponies roaming freely across the uplands and sometimes gathering in small herds by the roadside. They are still there but, in the last forty years, their numbers have declined tenfold and there are now less than 3000 ponies on Dartmoor. Although the ponies are still popular as children's mounts because of their gentle nature, they are no longer required for working on farms or down the coal mines of Wales. For these reasons, and because the Ministry of Agriculture does not grant subsidies for keeping ponies, there are few incentives for land owners to keep ponies on the moor.

Horses evolved from smaller, more primitive, horse-like mammals some sixty million years ago. It is not known for certain when the first horses came to Dartmoor but they were certainly well established by the time the first people arrived nearly 30 000 years ago, and the discovery of fossilized hoof prints dating from around the second millenium BC demonstrates that there continued to be ponies on the moor during the Bronze Age.

The original, pure-bred Dartmoor animals stood little more that 12 hands in height and ran wild on the moor, their tough constitutions enabling them to survive the harsh winters. They were used as pack and draught animals for transporting goods produced in local industries such as tin

mining, peat cutting, and the wool trade. In the nineteenth century, Dartmoor ponies were crossed with Shetlands to produce a strong, short-legged pony ideal for working in the confined space of the Welsh coal mines.

Although the ponies appear to enjoy the freedom of Dartmoor, they all belong to someone and, at the drift every year, the ponies are rounded up so that they can be claimed by their owners. The mares and foals then go back to the moor, while colts or any sick or old ponies are sold mainly to the pet food producers.

Visitors should always take a responsible attitude towards the ponies. If you feed them, it encourages the animals to come to the roadside and they may be killed by traffic. Similarly, rubbish left carelessly on the moor can easily choke or cut a pony — one report describes a pony which bled to death after being cut in the mouth by a ring pull from a soft drinks can.

rocks of largely very fossiliferous limestones in the Torquay/Brixham and Plymouth/Tavistock areas are gradually succeeded by slates of Upper Devonian age interspersed with some volcanic lavas. And in the Chudleigh area, for example, you can find nodular shales alternating with limestones which were probably deposited in the shallower water occurring over oceanic ridges. Further north again, and ignoring the great Dartmoor batholith of granite for the moment, rocks of Lower Carboniferous age form an arc around the northern edge of Dartmoor to Drewsteignton and thence around the eastern edge of the granite southwards from Christow to Cornwood. These rocks have been turned upside down and thrust, one layer upon another, as the Earth's crust heaved in later periods so that they are not easy to sort out. There are muddy, layered rocks, greyish-brown, silty slates, lime-rich silts, and sandy shales punctuated by nodules of limestone. Once again, volcanoes were active in the region during this period, and the rocks of Brent Tor and Sourton Tors are examples of Lower Carboniferous eruptions. To the west of Exeter, and stretching in a broad band north of Okehampton westwards as far as the North Devon/Cornish boundary, is a sequence of shales and sandstones dating from about 300 million years ago, and which have been given the name Crackington Formation, or Culm Measures, because of the presence of near coal-like material in some places.

The red-coloured beds containing sandstones, cobble-like conglomerates, and sharply angled stone-bearing breccias, as well as lime-rich marls have given their red coloration to the soils of an area stretching across east Devon from Torquay in the south, through Exeter and into north-east Devon and west Somerset. It has been difficult to attribute precise ages to these rocks, so that they have been given the name New Red Sandstone because of their similarity to the earlier continental formations of the Devonian Period known as the Old Red Sandstone. These rocks, laid down between about 270 and 225 million years ago, can be seen from examples such as the Budleigh Salterton Pebble Bed, and, on either side of the River Exe, the red deposits provide superb cliff scenery. There was volcanic activity during this period, too, with lava flows appearing at Dunchideock or in various localities in and around Exeter.

Deposits of a much more recent period in the Earth's history, a mere 30 million years or so ago, are to be found in the Bovey Tracey region where Oligocene clays have been worked for many years for use in the manufacture of earthenware, drainpipes, tiles, and bricks. Still younger rocks, which are sometimes exposed by storms to reveal fossilised forest remains, occur in Tor Bay at the mouth of the River Char.

The core of the whole south and mid-Devon area is Dartmoor and the heart of this is the granite. Dartmoor is one of five bosses or batholiths of granite which occur in the south-west peninsula, the others being Bodmin Moor, St Austell, Carnmellis, and Land's End. The Scilly Isles and a number of other smaller formations are also part of the same great granitic intrusion. The rugged grey tors of Dartmoor, shaped by time and weather into fantastic shapes, are the granite exposed. On closer inspection, the rock takes on a rough texture and a coarsely speckled appearance with flecks of brown and white mica glistening among the resistant quartz crystal and the regularly shaped and sometimes very large, pink or white crystals of feldspar. There are other minerals which go to make up the Dartmoor granite but these are the main ones.

Granite batholiths are huge bodies of igneous rock formed when two gigantic crustal plates (of which the surface of the Earth is composed like a three-dimensional jigsaw) are thrust together. The edge of one plate is forced down beneath the other and it is here, in the upper parts of the Earth's mantle, where the hot, liquid magma, which is the intrusion, rises upwards into the crust. Unlike the lava spewed out from a volcano, granitic magma cools and solidifies slowly, deep within the crust, so that its crystals have longer to grow and the rock is coarse grained. It is only the later erosion of the overlying rock which exposes the granite. In the case of Dartmoor, this process took place about 290 million years ago during the Carboniferous Period. Hot metallic vapours associated with the cooling magma found their way into crevices within the rock and it is these, when cooled, that provide the metal-bearing lodes of tin, copper, lead, zinc, silver, arsenic, and so on. And around the edge of the granite, the existing 'country rocks', as they are called, were buckled and heated to melting point by the hot batholith. The area around the granite, where the rocks have been changed in this way, is known as the 'metamorphic aureole'. It has added yet another facet to the already complex geology of the South Devon area.

If you look closely at the exposed rock on some of the tors, there seems almost to be two different kinds of granite: a coarse

Tin Mining

The presence of tin in and around Dartmoor is a direct consequence of the intrusion of the granite batholith. A batholith is a large body of igneous rock which formed in the Earth's mantle, cooled and crystallized in the crust, and was then thrust upwards, hot but essentially solid, unlike a volcanic eruption. In its wake came flows of hot vapours and liquids which found their way into the cracks and crevices in the already solidified granite and then cooled to form the tin-, copper-, and lead-rich minerals.

Cornish tin had been worked since the Bronze Age and tin is an essential ingredient of the metal which gave the period its name. Tin is also used in making pewter and solder but it is perhaps best known today for its use as a rust-resistant coat for steel containers — tin cans! It was not until the middle of the 1100s that tin was discovered on Dartmoor and the Cornish tinners were well able to provide the expertise to exploit the rich deposits. Much of the work was done by the streams and rivers washing over the exposed veins of tin-bearing ore. The debris was carried downstream until the flow of the water slowed and the heavy metalliferous stones were dropped on the outsides of bends in the rivers. All the miners had to do was to find the richest deposits and dig them out.

The next task was to crush the ore and, for both tasks, the power of water has been used at various times in the history of mining. Water wheels could be used to drive crushing mills and, once the ore had been crushed, the mud, sand, and other waste could be washed from the ore using a flow of water — sometimes speeded up by narrowing a stream. The resulting, cleaned ore was known as black tin. To produce tin metal, or white tin, the ore had to be smelted in furnaces which, at first, were simply fire pits.

From the various mines in and around the moor, the tin metal was sent by pack horse to Plympton, Chagford, Ashburton, or Tavistock. These were the so-called 'stannary towns' and it was around the industry that their importance was established. In these towns, the tin was tested for purity — 'coigned' — before being despatched mainly to London.

From an industry which, in the middle of the sixteenth century, was producing almost 200 tons of tin a year, it gradually declined until, by the early 1900s, it had gone completely. Interestingly, Cornish tin mining, which had an earlier start still seems to have a future provided the price of tin remains high.

material containing very large feldspar crystals, and a finer-grained, bluer rock. It has been suggested by two eminent geologists working on Dartmoor, that the magma was intruded as two separate sheets, with the finer-grained material forced into the coarse rock at a slightly later date. Most workers now, however, favour the idea that, as the magma cooled, it simply separated out into the two somewhat distinct forms.

The rocks described above, then, are the basic building blocks from which the South Devon landscape is constructed, a landscape which has been further modified over the aeons of time by the action of wind, water (rain and rivers), the sea, frost, and people. Readers familiar with the processes of weathering and erosion will have noticed a singular exception — ice — that great sculpting force which carved out so many valleys, chiselled away at mountains, and changed the flow of rivers some 10 000 years ago and more. But the ice sheets of the Pleistocene Period did not reach the south-west peninsula, although the region must have been subjected to near-Arctic conditions where Arctic mammals must have grazed on tundra-like vegetation.

Long before the glaciers retreated from the British Isles some ten millennia ago, causing a substantial rise in the sea level, it seems likely that the group of islands which is now Britain and Ireland was joined to continental Europe by what is sometimes described as a land bridge. This would have allowed primitive humans to have made their way into southern England perhaps 200 000 years ago although the evidence for their presence is scant. Leaping forward in time some 170 000 years, stone and bone tools dating from between 20 000 and 30 000 years ago have been discovered in Kent's Cavern in Torquay, although it was not until about 17 000 years ago that humans were venturing on to Dartmoor; at Postbridge, for example, flint tools of the Middle Stone Age have been found. Both the Kent's Cavern discoveries and those on Dartmoor seem to provide evidence that these prehistoric peoples lived a nomadic hunting and gathering lifestyle and used caves, such as the extensive cavern system at Torquay, as a temporary home when the weather deteriorated.

It is from the Neolithic or New Stone Age period, between about 6000 and 4000 years ago, that evidence of human activity becomes more abundant. These people probably came from northern France and settled in areas near Totnes, Sidmouth, and Honiton. They must have wandered on to Dartmoor, if only to hunt, for flint arrowheads have been found here although there is no evidence of their pottery or living places on the moor from this period. It has to be admitted, however, that, if there were farming folk living here then, they may well have built in timber of which little trace is likely to remain. On the other hand, it seems that they must have been well organized in pursuit of their quarries for the forest of Dartmoor had already been fired (as shown by fossil pollen evidence) to drive game ahead of the advancing flames and into the hunters' clutches. It seems that the moor was also used for burying the dead at this time, and various burial chambers, such as that at Spinster's Rock, can be seen dotted around the region.

The Bronze Age came to Britain, between 4000 and 2500 years ago, in the shape of the Beaker Folk, a new immigration from Europe and probably from the area which is now Spain. The period gets its name from the fact that these people had discovered the means of making a durable metallic alloy from copper and tin, both of which were abundant on Dartmoor. And the people are so called because, in the round barrows in which they buried their dead, the corpse was accompanied by characteristically shaped and decorated pottery. On Dartmoor, however, little now remains of the bronze tools and weapons which they fashioned largely because the acid soil quickly corrodes the metal. The Beaker Folk were a well-organized, pastoral people, and it is to them that Dartmoor owes its stone rows and circles as well as the enclosed settlements, such as the well-known Grimspound, where people and domestic stock could be protected from marauding wild animals. J R L Anderson, author of *The Oldest Road: the Ridgeway*, proposes that it was not only stone circles and hut circles which were built by these

---

Stone rows, standing stones, and burial chambers

There are at least 500 sites on Dartmoor, such as Drizzlecombe or Merrivale, where stone constructions, erected between about 3500 and 1500 BC, have been discovered. This is the time of the New Stone Age or Neolithic although, because of the scale of the stone constructions that have been found, it is also referred to as the Megalithic or 'great stone' period. Stone constructions, such as the remains of the enclosed hut circle of Grimspound, belong to a later period of building during the Bronze Age.

Essentially, there are two main types of stone structures from this period: various kinds of tombs; and stone rows and circles. The tombs themselves are also mainly of two types. The large, chamber tombs, such as that at the so-called Spinster's Rock near Drewsteignton, may have been used for successive burials, perhaps of complete families, and the stone remains which can be seen today were probably covered by a mound of earth to resemble the more familiar barrows found in other parts of the country. Later, single, stone burial coffins were placed in the ground and covered with a stone slab. These are usually referred to as kists and, as time went by, they became smaller until, eventually, they were only big enough to hold a cremation urn as well as some of the deceased's effects.

The rows and circles are often to be seen close to burial chambers and were once thought to have held ritual significance. Since Professor Alexander Thom has carried out his studies into these stone monuments throughout Britain and Europe, it is now widely believed that they are prehistoric 'astro-calendars' enabling the people, who were by now settled farmers, to predict important events in the growing seasons.

The remains of the enclosed hut circle at Grimspound.

The 'Ice Age' Returns!

One of the strangest of Dartmoor industries was ice-making! Standing almost 1500 feet above sea level, the heights of Sourton Tors would guarantee freezing temperatures in all but the mildest of winters, And here, too, there are supplies of fresh water close to the sources of the River Okement, so Sourton Tors is thought to have been the site of an ice works.

In these days of cheap refrigeration and when almost every home has its deep freeze, it is hard to imagine a time when people might go to such extraordinary lengths to make ice. But in a county where even the winters were mild and where one of the main industries was fishing, a supply of ice to keep the fish fresh was vital. During the winter, the naturally low temperatures close to the peaks of Sourton Tors were exploited to make the ice which could then be stored deep underground until it was needed. The problem then was to get the ice from its source to the place where it was wanted — Plymouth which, even as the crow flies, is a distance of almost 25 miles. Needless to say, by the time the ice reached its destination, much of it was water, and ice-making on Dartmoor did not enjoy a long or prosperous career.

people. He claims that the hill fortresses which form a north-facing line of defence along the Ridgeway in Wiltshire and Berkshire, for example, were also of Beaker origin, and were therefore earlier than the officially sanctioned Iron Age date.

About 2750 years ago, the technique of smelting iron and forging tools and weapons from the metal was perfected. Iron is a much harder metal than bronze and takes a sharp edge more effectively. Consequently, it would have been a comparatively easy matter for warriors armed with iron swords to supplant their Bronze Age predecessors although, in fact, the change from bronze to iron was a gradual one. Once again, the official line is that the hillforts found at such places as Cadbury, Prestonbury near Drewsteignton, Cranbrook Castle, and Hembury Castle near Buckfastleigh, were of Iron Age construction. Remains of an iron smelting house and a workshop have also been found near Kes Tor on Dartmoor.

The Roman legions first set foot on British soil in 55 BC only to leave again and then return the following year, this time to stay. Five years later, Roman influence had arrived in Devon. Their first garrison was at Seaton but Exeter soon became the Roman centre for their further invasion westwards with communications both by road and by sea from the east. In about 200 AD Exeter was fortified by massive walls to protect its trading interests and, to this day, the centre of Exeter is still essentially a walled city. As the great Roman empire decayed, Rome was obliged to withdraw its legions from the outpost of Britain to defend lands nearer home from Barbarian incursions, so that Devon and its settlements were left to themselves. Like so much of Britain, with the withdrawal of the Roman organization, culture, and systems of government, Devon's history during the so-called Dark Ages is swathed in mystery. It is during this era that King Arthur was thought to have held court in neighbouring Somerset.

Although they had been in Britain for some time, it was not until the seventh and eighth centuries that the Saxon invaders found their way westwards and Devon became part of the shire county system which had already been established elsewhere. This was also the start of the pattern of settlement of Dartmoor which continued through medieval times and is still in evidence today, although few traces of actual Saxon construction survive. From the ninth to the early part of the eleventh century, the Danes occupied large stretches of Britain and sought to invade others. Wessex was a bastion of Saxon resistance and, even though Exeter, for example, fell to the Vikings in the latter quarter of the ninth century, King Alfred was quick to drive them out again and it was not until 1003 that Exeter was overrun once again. These were unsettled times and Britain was unknowingly awaiting the coming of the Normans to re-establish an order which had been lacking since the last Romans left the country.

In 1067 King William I brought his armies to Exeter and, by negotiation rather than by bloodshed, Norman rule was established firmly in the west country. This was despite the fact that the mother of the last of the Saxon kings had rallied the support of the Devon people to resist these latest invading forces. Evidence of William's way of controlling his subjects is clear enough in Exeter in the shape of the remains of Rougemont Castle built at the highest part of the existing wall and still housing Exeter's local courts. As if to confirm his rule in this more remote part of his realm, William built more castles such as the ones, whose remains can still be seen, at Totnes and Okehampton. In

Dartmoor Crossing!

Although it was first published almost ninety years ago by the Western Morning News, the famous Crossing's Guide to Dartmoor remains in print to this day, the modern version based on the second, 1912 edition. Many people still believe that the Guide continues to be the best topographical book of its kind that has ever been published about the Moor.

Born in Plymouth in 1847, William Crossing was a Devon man through and through. He spent his early years in the city learning about the country-side (including Dartmoor where the family spent their holidays) until he ran away to sea and ended up in Canada for a brief period. He soon returned to his birth place and worked for his father, running the family mill in South Brent. It seems that his other interests, such as drama, poetry, and of course, Dartmoor took most of his attention and energy so that, needless to say, the business suffered and eventually the mill was closed. By now Crossing was married and he decided that his pen should be the instrument of their fortunes. It was not to be,

however, and although he produced books and numerous articles, he almost ended up in the workhouse. Wandering on the Moor, talking to the moorland folk, and learning of their ancient customs continued to delight him although as a result of the harsh weather he encountered, his health deteriorated to a point where he could hardly write.

Various notables, including the then Lord Clifford, came to Crossing's aid, and he was able to continue work on his Guide to Dartmoor. Illustrated by Philip Guy Stevens, the first edition was published in May 1909. William Crossing returned to Plymouth where he was to die in Cross Park Nursing Home in 1928 at the age of eighty-one. With his wife, who died seven years before him, William Crossing is buried in the churchyard of Mary Tavy. In 1952, a slate tablet was attached to the house in which William Crossing lived as a memorial to a man who, more than any other, has given us such a powerful insight into the geography and culture of one of southern England's most dramatic places.

1086, or thereabouts, King William commissioned the writing of the Domesday Book to grant and record ownership, extent, and value of all the lands of England. Domesday records, for example, that the population of the whole of Devon was about 60 000 souls and that there were almost forty manors whose lands lay on Dartmoor. One such manor was that of Hound Tor which belonged to the Abbot of

Tavistock. Close by the tor itself, visitors can look at the obvious remains of a stone-built medieval village, dating from between 1200 and 1350, which probably stood on the site of an earlier wattle and turf settlement, and which was abandoned some time during the fourteenth century. Hound Tor village was probably deserted because the climate of Dartmoor became too harsh although it is possible that the

Devonshire Clotted Cream

With its mild, damp climate and good soil, it is not surprising that the lush lands of Devon should provide such rich pasture for Channel Island dairy cattle thereby leading to the production of one of Devon's most famous exports, clotted cream. What other activity can conjure more completely the atmosphere of a Devon holiday than a Devonshire cream tea in a welcoming farmhouse setting where tables groan under plates of scones, lashings of cream, strawberry jam, and a pot of tea.

If you are willing to take the time and trouble, you can bring back memories of your Devon holiday by making cream at home. Buy some Jersey or Guernsey milk (or a mixture of the

two) and leave it to stand. In summer, twelve hours should be enough but you should leave the milk for twenty-four hours in winter time. Then stand your bowl of milk over a pan of water and heat the pan on the stove — heat it gently and make sure you do not allow the water to boil. Let the bowl of milk stand over the hot water until a thick, creamy crust has appeared on the top of the milk. Now just store it in a cold larder until the next day when you can skim off the delicious clotted cream.

Cream is not the only food for which Devon is justly famous. Honey, scrumpy, sea food, various meats including venison, fine vegetables, and even wine are just some of the delights waiting to tempt tourist gourmets.

Rabbit Warrening

Few mammals are so familiar to the British as the ubiquitous rabbit despite the deadly disease, myxomatosis, which was once introduced to control their numbers in the wild. But rabbits are not, in fact, native to the British Isles. They were once confined to the Iberian peninsula and parts of North Africa; it was the Norman invaders who brought rabbits to Britain in the eleventh century for they had already acquired a taste for their meat. And rabbits are more efficient converters of vegetable matter into protein than cattle, sheep, or goats.

As in many other parts of Britain, on Dartmoor rabbits were looked upon as an important source of fresh meat. Consequently, they were actively 'farmed' or warrened. In various parts of the moor remains of the old warrens can still be seen, and many place names and houses, such as Ditsworthy Warren or the Warren House Inn, reflect the activity's former importance. To encourage the rabbits to live and breed in a given area, the warreners would build

artificial rabbit warrens by digging a pit or a ditch, filling it with stones, and then building up a bank or mound of earth on which grass would be allowed to grow. The rabbits in the warrens were prevented from straying and protected from marauding foxes or weasels by stone walls and by the vigilance of the warrener who lived in the nearby warrener's house. It was his task to set traps, made from the most easily available material, granite, and to catch them for slaughter.

Ditsworthy Warren.

arrival of the Black Death in England in 1348 hastened the destruction of this and other villages in the area. But not all traces of medieval occupation on Dartmoor have been so erased; the tenement farm at Pizwell, near Postbridge, for example, dates from 1260 and is still occupied to this day.

Throughout the Middle Ages, and until the sixteenth century, two industries created the wealth and provided the stability of South Devon and Dartmoor — cloth and, later, tin. It was during this period that many of the churches, grand expressions of religious belief, were either built or enlarged on sites of earlier worship. St Pancras Church at Widecombe, for example, is a fitting tribute to the tin miners who worked in the area and is often called the 'cathedral of the moor'. And it is around tin mining that four of the Dartmoor towns, Plympton, Chagford, Ashburton, and Tavistock, achieved their status. To be exported, the tin had to be taken to a port and, for the most part, it was Plympton, Exeter, Dartmouth, and Morwellham the served the purpose. Exeter not only played its part as a port, but was also a centre for the Devon cloth trade which, in medieval times, was widespread in Devon with full-

ing mills wherever there was a good flow of water.

With so much coastline, so many sheltered bays and deep-water estuaries, it is hardly surprising that South Devon's maritime history should be such a long and important one. Dartmouth had been a harbour for thousands of years and, in the twelfth century, sent its ships to join the crusades. It was in the fourteenth and fifteenth centuries, however, that its importance grew as fleets were sent out to trade in wine with Bordeaux. A century or two later it was for fishing and the fruit trade that the boats set sail from Dartmouth although the port had already made its contribution to the Royal Navy fleet sent out to meet the Spanish Armada in 1588. By the beginning of the eighteenth century, sail was beginning to give way to steam-driven ships and, once again, Dartmouth found its place as a re-fuelling port. Finally, in 1905, Britannia Royal College was built in Dartmouth and, today, the port is one of South Devon's centres for leisure sailing.

This pattern, described for Dartmouth, is reflected in many of Devon's coastal towns although fishing boats still do go out from places such as Brixham and Beer.

The Pilgrim Fathers

Setting out from Plymouth in 1620 for a little-known destination on what must have seemed to them like the other side of the world, the young men, women, and children who embarked on this voyage, have come down through history as heroes. At the place where they climbed aboard their little ship, The Mayflower, there is a plaque to their memory, the so-called Mayflower Steps. And, at Bayard's Cove near Dartmouth, there is a small plaque which marks the point where passengers en route for their embarkation place, stopped off. It was not always so.

The Puritan Movement in England despised Roman Catholicism and sought to cleanse the Protestant religion of what it regarded as high church, Latin ritual. They were austere people who disapproved of any of the pleasures of the flesh, and as a consequence, they were often denied any kind of religious freedom during the reign of James I. To escape injustice, as well as heavy taxes, some Puritans exiled themselves to the strictly Protestant Netherlands but others felt that, by fleeing to Europe, they would lose their English identity. There was only one place to go, it seemed, where these people could remain both English and Puritan, North America. Thus they set sail no doubt fearful and, at the same time, full of hope for their new world. Quite by chance, they landed at a place which had already been named Plymouth.

Exeter, of course, is no longer a port although Plymouth, whose maritime history needs no description, still sends out its ferries and ships of war. Little of the old Plymouth remains and it has been substantially rebuilt since the end of World War II — its use as a naval dockyard ensured its attention by Nazi bombers even though the rest of Devon escaped comparatively unscathed.

Today, because of Devon's beautiful countryside, charming villages, well-organized visitor facilities, and an atmosphere steeped in history as well as bathed in sunshine, tourism must rate as Devon's most important industry. But the tourist authorities are not resting on their laurels; during 1987, for example, the West Country Tourist Board compiled a list of possible projects which might be submitted to the EEC for a new programme of job creation. These included the Tarka Trail Project and the Dartmoor National Park Interpretation Plan proposals. Despite temptingly cheap package tours to parts of the world where the weather is more reliable, there seems little doubt that South Devon and Dartmoor has a guaranteed future as one of Britain's foremost holiday centres.

The Dartmoor Commons Act 1985

The Dartmoor Commons Act, which was passed by Parliament in 1985, was proposed jointly by the National Park Authority and the Commoners' Association almost thirty years after the declaration of a partnership between the commoners and the Authority. One of its most important aspects is that public access to the common land in the Park is legally, rather than traditionally, safeguarded and the behaviour of those members of the public who take advantage of that legal right are also subject to bylaws to ensure that the interests of the Park and its inhabitants (wild, domestic, and human) are also cared for. In general terms, the aim of the act is to improve the management of the Park for the long-term future of the owners and commoners, and so that the ecology of a tract of land which the public at large wishes to enjoy can be at the least, protected, and at best, enriched.

Just over 40 per cent of the unenclosed land, some 99 000 acres, of the Dartmoor National Park consists of three main classes: the Forest of Dartmoor (in this context the word 'forest' refers generally to an area of wooded grounds and pastures set apart for game and generally belonging to the sovereign), the Commons of Dartmoor, and various other commons attached to manors. These areas are the Dartmoor Commons owned by sixty different landowners and offering registered grazing, firewood, and domestic stone and peat-cutting rights to 1500 commoners. It is vital that these people should have their rights safeguarded as well as allowing the Park to be used for recreational purposes by visitors to the area.

Some Devon Worthies

Charles Kingsley (1819-75). The vicar, who was both poet and author, was born into the clergy as it were, in that his father was the curate at the Church of St Mary the Virgin at the time, and Charles entered the world in the vicarage. The two works for which Kingsley is perhaps best known are The Water Babies *and* Westward Ho!, *part of the latter written during a stay at the Royal Hotel near Bideford in North Devon. Interestingly, the holiday resort of Westward Ho!, near Appledore in North Devon, took its name from the book rather than the other way round as is more usual.*

Sir Walter Raleigh (1552-1618) was born in the imposing farmhouse of Hayes Barton at East Budleigh near Budleigh Salterton. He was known to enjoy the patronage of Queen Elizabeth. Although he was an author of some repute, Raleigh is best known as an explorer of the New World, setting sail from Plymouth in 1584 to arrive on the shores of what is now Carolina. It is commonly believed that it was Raleigh who brought two important commodities to England on his return from the Americas — tobacco and the potato.

Among other famous names, from or associated with South Devon, are: Samuel Taylor Coleridge (1772-1834) the poet and philosopher who was born in Ottery St Mary and is best known for such ballads as Kubla Khan *and* The Ancient Mariner; *Sir Arthur Conan Doyle ((1859-1930) who set his tale,* The Hound of the Baskervilles, *on Dartmoor; and Agatha Christie who once lived by the River Dart and loved South Devon.*

Sir Francis Drake (1540-96). Born at Crowndale, about a mile south of Tavistock, Francis Drake is best remembered for supposedly having suggested that his encounter with the Spanish Armada could wait until he finished his game of bowls on Plymouth Hoe. He was, in fact, a pirate as well as an Admiral in Queen Elizabeth I's navy, and a sailor who successfully completed a voyage around the world — setting off from Plymouth in his ship, the Golden Hind, in 1577. When he returned to Devon, he bought Buckland Abbey from Sir Richard Grenville who had saved the thirteenth-century monastery from destruction by converting it into a country house. The best-known statue of Drake is on Plymouth Hoe but there is another in Plymouth Road in Tavistock which is, in fact, the original from which the Plymouth memorial was replicated

Sir Humphrey Gilbert (1539-83) may be regarded as the first English colonizer of America with his occupation of Newfoundland. He was a half-brother to Sir Walter Raleigh and lived in Compton Castle at Marldon near Paignton, a fortified manor house which is still the home of the Gilbert family although it is owned and managed by the National Trust.

Top: *the statue of Sir Francis Drake at Tavistock.* Below: *Compton Castle, home of Sir Humphrey Gilbert.*

Natural History of South Devon and Dartmoor

Devon is a very fortunate county in that it still retains much of the richness and variety of wildlife with which it has long been blessed. The many threats posed by the twentieth century have not yet done to Devon what they have done to many counties of England — most notably in the east — and it is still possible to walk among ancient woodlands or cross open expanses of moorland.

Despite the differences between the austere and open expanses of the moor and the 'cosier' patchwork of fields and settlements to the south of it, Dartmoor and South Devon are, in many ways, linked. Many of the rivers which reach the sea along the south coast, for example, have their origins on Dartmoor. Rivers, such as the Avon, Erme, Plym, and Yealm often rise no more than 20 miles from the sea as the crow flies and, in the distance, they descend about 1500 feet. Consequently, they are fast flowing and, because they rise among the moorland peats, they are acidic. They hold a head of native brown trout which seldom grow very large as the rivers do not offer a rich diet. Ironically, the rivers do afford ideal spawning grounds on their many clean gravel beds, which means that even more trout are competing for a very limited food supply. Walk quietly by any South Devon river and you will see these fishes, holding against the current and waiting to move out from their station behind a rock or on the edge of an eddy to seize passing morsels.

The lords of these rivers are undoubtedly the migratory fishes which, seeking their food elsewhere, return to the rivers of their birth to spawn. The salmon has the longer journey, leaving its native river as a smolt to travel to the waters around Greenland where it feasts on shrimps and other marine life before venturing back to complete the 'cycle'. Sea trout, on the other hand, travel no further than the south coast where they, too, grow quickly on the rich pickings. During the summer, the rivers are often too low for them to 'run' so they wait at the mouth and then, with the first floods of autumn, they move swiftly into the higher reaches to spawn.

Dartmoor and South Devon are also linked traditionally by agriculture. The land of South Devon has been fashioned by many hundreds of years of human use, and the small hedgerow and Devon Bank enclosed fields between moor and sea reflect farming practice oriented towards animal husbandry. Dartmoor itself has always been used for rough summer grazing, the animals being driven up on to the moor in spring and then brought down again in autumn. It is grazing by these animals which has produced the characteristic short-turfed expanses of Dartmoor; without the stock, the moor would have reverted to the woodland with which it was covered before the arrival of people perhaps 5000 years ago.

Sheep are the most numerous grazing animals on the moor. Most of them are the Scottish black face, chosen for their hardiness, because Dartmoor winters can be brutal. These animals lead an almost feral existence, often being brought down off the moor only for a short time each year. The numbers of skulls and bones encountered when walking on Dartmoor bears macabre testimony to the hard living which they endure.

To characterize and catalogue the animals and plants of so considerable and varied an area is a daunting task but, broadly, there are three areas to consider: Dartmoor itself, the lowlands of South Devon, and the coast.

Dartmoor

Dartmoor is the largest and highest area of upland in southern Britain. Standing, as it does, in the face of the prevailing and moisture-laden westerly winds, it is very wet and relatively cold, but its southern latitude ameliorates the effects of this so that its plants and animals are an interesting mix of species found much further to the north and to the south. Its bird population, for instance, includes breeding dunlin, which are at the very southern limit of their range, and breeding woodlarks at their northern extremity.

The high moor consists almost entirely of blanket bog, thick layers of peat made up of organic matter in which the decomposition has been arrested by the cold, wet conditions. The plant life here is relatively limited, consisting of heathers, coarse grasses, and specialized plants such as bog cotton and the lovely bog asphodel, with its delicate, orange-yellow flowers on leafless stems adding a surprising beauty to the harsh landscape. Lower down, where the ground is drier, tracts of grass and heather moorland roll down from the tors; it is here that stands of gorse, with their vivid yellow flowers, can be found. The gorse is one of the few plants which can dare to be erect in a landscape where grazing animals are always foraging, its vicious spines provid-

Birds of Dartmoor: the buzzard (top), skylark (centre), and the wheatear (bottom).

raven may well go kronking by. In summer, skylarks are always evident from their song, though spotting the tiny dot against the sky is often impossible. Pipits, too, are seen everywhere, flying up and then 'parachuting' back to earth with their wings pulled back behind them. Perhaps the most characteristic species is the wheatear, of which Dartmoor has the largest breeding population in northern Europe. These birds, which flit from one granite outcrop to another, are easily spotted by the flash of the white rump. The old country name was 'whitearse' — it was the Victorian naturalists who sanitized the name into its modern form!

It is the grazing animals which maintain the moorland's characteristic flora. With them, and with the traditional management of regular 'swaling' (burning) associated with them, it retains the mixture of heathers and grasses on which the animals feed.

Many of the grassy lower areas of the moor have been invaded by bracken, its spread aided by past cultivation of parts of the moor which has produced conditions entirely to its liking. In summer, its fronds grow quickly from about June, reaching heights of 6 to 8 feet in places; in winter, it lies, wet and brown, blanketing the ground and making it very difficult for other plant species to compete. Control of the bracken is a serious management problem because it has deep underground rhizomes which are unaffected by burning; once established, it is very difficult to eradicate.

Bracken has its value for wildlife, however, especially where occasional rowans and hawthorns have managed to rise above it and establish themselves. Here is a haven for the whinchat and stonechat, the yellowhammer and the redstart; here, too, is cover for some of the larger mammals, such as foxes and badgers.

On the edges of the moor and on the sides of the deep valleys, cut by rivers as they leave the high moorland plateau, can be found the best of Dartmoor's woodlands. Much of this land, especially on the valley sides, has never been claimed for cultivation, being too steep to plough, and so the woods found here have their beginnings in the ancient woodlands which once covered the whole area. The woods have always been managed for their timber, both for domestic supply (firewood, fence posts, house timbers) and also to produce the charcoal needed to smelt tin which was mined from medieval times until quite recently.

Management was by coppicing, which means that 'maiden' trees — mostly sessile oak — are cut close to the ground and

ing it with a clever and very effective defence. The ubiquitous tormentil, on the other hand, survives by keeping its head down, its tiny, four-petalled, yellow flowers clinging to the close-cropped, grassy surface.

The bird life of these high, open spaces is particularly striking. The buzzard, which has made a remarkable comeback all over Devon, can often be seen wheeling overhead, and the huge black silhouette of a the 'stool' is then left to produce multiple shoots which are regularly harvested. Worked in this way, the trees remain productive for hundreds of years. Once management ceases, they grow on to produce the typical multiple-stemmed specimens found in these woodlands.

Coppice was by rotation, so that there was a full range of woodland habitats always available. In newly cleared areas, flowers such as primrose, bluebell, and violet flourished, eventually to be shaded out by the tangle of shoots which provide cover and nest sites for birds and for that charming and endangered mammal, the dormouse. The woods are also home to a kaleidoscope of butterflies such as the speckled wood, silver-washed fritillary, and the ringlet.

No broad survey can do justice to the extraordinary diversity of species and habitats which make up Dartmoor, particularly because, within the broad range of moorland 'types', there are many local variations, such as old mine workings and quarries, which support their own particular community of species, including the striking ring ousel, a bird which looks like a large blackbird with a white collar and which frequents heathery gullies. There is, however, one 'localized' habitat which is of particular interest: valley bogs. Unlike blanket bogs, which derive all of their water from rainfall, valley bogs have a slow through-flow of water which makes available larger quantities of 'migrant' nutrients. They are, therefore, able to support a whole range of water-loving plants not found elsewhere on the moor.

These bogs show up bright green against the surrounding moorland, and the 'canopy' of plant growth is so dense that it is often possible to walk out on to such 'featherbeds' and feel the earth moving beneath your feet! The most spectacular plant found here is the sundew, which glows a reddish green. Its leaves secrete a sticky fluid on the ends of hairs, which trap insects and then curve inwards to hold them. In this way, the plant is able to supplement its nutrient supply.

The other glory of the valley bogs is the proliferation of dragonflies which come in a wide range of colours and an assortment

The grassy lower areas of the moor, having been invaded by bracken, are now havens for the stonechat (top left), redstart (top right), the fox (bottom left), and the badger (bottom right).

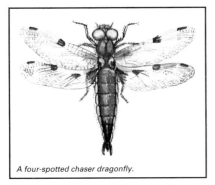

A four-spotted chaser dragonfly.

of spots and stripes. They revel in such exotic names as the four-spotter chaser and the keeled skimmer.

South Devon

The area south of Dartmoor, bordered on one side by the River Tamar and on the other by the Exe, consists of a semicircle of lowland which, with the inclusion of south-east Devon to the Axe, makes up an area which has always been dominated by agriculture. The patchwork Devon scene has been built up over thousands of years, the wildlife diversifying and growing richer as the range of agricultural management expanded. Ironically, it is the modern reversal of this trend, and the movement towards intensive and efficient land use, which most threatens nature in Devon. While the eye is still met with a landscape of rolling pastures, many of these fields have been 'improved' by draining, reseeding, and fertilizing to the point where their value for wildlife is minimal.

It is in the parts of the landscape which have survived the modernizing onslaught that the wildlife interest must be sought. There are still traditional hay meadows whose flowery pastures contain scabious, ox-eye daisies, a variety of orchids, hay rattle, and the whole range of plants associated with land which has seldom seen the plough and has never been subjected to modern fertilizers. To this rich habitat come insects of all kinds, the most spectacular being the many butterflies which come to sip the nectar of the various flowers and to use them as food plants for their caterpillars. Marbled white, small copper, meadow brown, common blue — over traditional grassland these can be found adance in numbers which take the breath away. The rich crop of seeds and fruits attracts different species of small mammals, making these fields prime hunting land for such birds as the kestrel and the barn owl, whose numbers have declined alarmingly in the south of Devon.

As the fields are improved, so hedge-rows and field banks are often grubbed up to make working the land more efficient. Despite this, they remain a very important and prominent feature of the agricultural landscape of South Devon, and, running as they do between the improved fields, offer sanctuary for a very distinct community of plants and animals.

The basis for the hedgerow is usually hazel, beech, blackthorn, or hawthorn which has been made into a dense hedge by layering; this involves cutting part way through growing stems and 'layering' them horizontally. The result is not only impenetrable to stock but it is so thick that it can keep out fierce winter winds, providing a secure overwintering site for many insects and a haven for birds and small mammals. Sadly, even where such hedgerows are retained, they are now more usually managed by using a mechanical flail which results in a much less windproof end product. On the bank beneath the hedge, campion, stinging nettle, and primroses commonly abound together with wild strawberries and herb Robert. Through it weave the climbers: the ubiquitous bramble, various vetches and bed-

To the traditional meadows still found in South Devon, come insects of all kinds, including the marbled white (top), small copper (centre), and common blue (bottom) butterflies.

With the rich crop of seeds and fruits attracting a variety of small mammals, the fields of South Devon become prime hunting grounds for such birds as kestrel (left) and barn owl (right).

straws, and the beautifully scented honeysuckle. In the breeding season, dozens of species of birds find in the dense tangle an ideal nesting site while, all around, the fruits and insects provide a rich larder from which to raise their young.

Where the bank is supported by a wall, members of the aptly named stonecrop family can be found, such as English stonecrop and navelwort which carries its bell-like flowers on long spikes. On warm days, lizards bask on the stones sunning themselves, as does the wall brown butterfly, while in patches of bare earth around them are found colonies of mining bees and wasps.

Not all of the South Devonshire countryside has been turned over to farming, of course. Patches of ancient woodland remain, often containing rare species, such as the heath lobelia, while the show of wild daffodils in Dunsford Woods (managed by the Devon Wildlife Trust) is the finest in the south-west. But the most striking 'open' habitat in the area is its lowland heath, a type of habitat which is threatened internationally, and with which Devon is well blessed, particularly in the area to the east of Exeter. Sadly, lowland heath is land which developers and planners have long regarded as 'waste', and large areas have disappeared beneath concrete, tarmac, and buildings. Heath has developed, again in part shaped by human use of it, on the sandy and gravelly soils of lowland Britain. Like the high moorland, it is characterized by heathers and gorse with patches of cotton-grass and purple moor grass, and, while lowland heath is relatively poor in species of plants, it is a haven for a vast array of spiders and insects, and for all six species of native reptiles. It also boasts populations of rare and threatened birds such as the nightjar and the Dartford warbler, whose rufous chest, blue-grey back, and long tail make it a striking creature perched atop a gorse bush. A walk across Woodbury Common (east of Exeter and on **Tour 1**)

will convey the flavour of this interesting habitat.

South Devon also has a third type of habitat, known as maritime heath because it is found on exposed headlands which are subject to the influence of the strong, salty, Atlantic winds. On the fringes of these heaths will be found clumps of sea campion and thrift. Berry Head Country Park ★ (near Brixham ★) is the largest exposure of Devonian-age limestone in Britain and, in addition to the common species associated with maritime heath, it has its own rarities, such as white rock rose and goldilocks aster.

South Devon is well endowed with rivers, many of them rising on Dartmoor as was mentioned earlier, although the Exe snakes its way south all the way from Exmoor. Typically, they are acidic rivers which, flowing swiftly to the sea, do not build up the beds of sediment necessary for a lush bankside vegetation. This limits the fish population to the native brown trout and to the eels, sea trout, and salmon which run up them. Those rivers to the east of the region which do not rise on Dartmoor, however, have a more varied population including coarse fishes such as roach and dace.

It is the populations of plants and animals which have adapted to life by the waterside which make these rivers so interesting. Their banks are lined with willow and alder; pondskaters and whirligig beetles patrol the surface where the flow is reduced; dragonflies hover and dart along the bank; and the ephemeral mayflies hatch, lay their eggs, and die. All these are food for the swooping swallow, the darting wagtails, and, after dark, for the bats which work their way up and down just over the water. It is here that the iridescent, azure-blue flash of the kingfisher is often seen; here, too, that the dipper sits and bobs on rocks in midstream before plunging beneath the surface to walk along the bottom looking for food.

If, however, there is one creature which is romantically connected with the Devon riverside, it is the otter. The largest populations of otters are on the rivers in the north of the county, and, of course, populations everywhere suffered substantial setbacks in previous decades as a result of the use of pesticides which entered the rivers' food chains and were concentrated in massive doses in the predatory animals at the tops of the chains. Now, fortunately, the otter is making a comeback on some rivers in the south, though the chances of seeing this shy and secretive creature are

The mouth of the River Teign at Teignmouth – particularly good for wading birds.

very poor. Most people who think they have seen an otter have, in fact, seen a mink of which there are substantial feral colonies in Devon because of an escape from a fur farm in the 1950s.

The coast

The south-west coast of Devon is characterized by coastal cliffs worn sheer by Atlantic attack, with many of the small bays rocky and inaccessible. To the south-east, however, which is a much more protected coastline, there are far more beaches, both of sand and of stones. And, within this broad framework, there is a great deal of variety.

Estuaries

For every Devon river, there is an estuary — and in one particular case, there is an estuary with no river! The Kingsbridge ★ estuary, which drives deep into the southern promontory of Devon, is fed by the merest trickles of streams, and consequently the aquatic life in most of it is purely marine. This means that creatures which are normally obliged to live out at sea can enter the estuary and seek shelter from the severe wave action around the point, making the area unique among Devon's estuaries. The remainder of the estuaries have the 'grading' of salinity usually associated with the meeting of fresh and sea water but, because they are almost all 'rias' or drowned valleys (reclaimed by sea levels which were once much lower), and because they carry relatively small volumes of fresh water, they are more saline than most. The Dartmoor rivers particularly have small estuaries, with the sea pushing sediment up into them rather than them driving banks of sediment out into the sea, but some of the rivers of the east (notably the Teign and Exe) do have rather broader estuaries with more mud and sand banks making them particularly attractive to wading birds. It is here that the elegant black-and-white avocets overwinter, along with other

waders such as bar-tailed and black-tailed godwit, turnstone and greenshank. They also attract huge flocks of ducks and geese, especially wigeon which come here in enormous numbers.

Estuaries are the most biologically productive of all temperate habitats, and the sand banks and rocks, mud flats and shallows teem with life. Walk along any sand bank at low tide and you are likely to see casts of lugworms, the largest of the many marine worms which are an important part of the diets of wading birds with long, probing bills. Kick at the surface of the sand or gravel and you will find cockles lying buried just beneath the surface; splash in the shallows and small flatfishes, sandeels, prawns, and blennies will scat-

Around the coast from Kingswear, at Froward Cove, the coastal path leads the eye to the offshore rocks.

ter before your feet; lift a carpet of kelp (don't forget to put it back) and sand hoppers begin a demented dance in search of new cover. And, to feed on all this richness, there are gulls and terns, herons and shelduck, which give way, as the tide rises, to predatory fishes, such as the bass, which hunt across the now submerged banks.

The shore
Beaches have a natural fascination for young and old alike. Whether sandy, like Bantham or Blackpool beaches, or stony, like those around Budleigh Salterton ★, they reveal, to the interested eye, a good deal about life beneath the surface of the sea. Rock pools contain all sorts of molluscs, such as winkles, whelks, mussels, and limpets. Look at any dense colony of limpets and you will see circular depres-

The Buckfast Bee

From sheep, the monks of Buckfast Abbey, have turned their attention to making tonic wine and to bee-keeping. The head bee-keeper is Brother Adam who, at the age of over ninety, has been at his post for some seventy years at the time of going to press. Bee-keeping has been carried out at the Abbey for generations and, in the wall by the lawn at the South Gate, it is still possible to see the holes or recesses where the ancient basketwork hives, or skeps, were placed. But it is Brother Adam who has put Buckfast on the apiarist's map. He has spent his life, engaged in genetic research, to breed a new kind of bee, the 'Buckfast Bee', which is not aggressive and which produces a fine-quality honey. The Buckfast bee rarely swarms and, most importantly for bee-keepers, it is not subject to disease.

The queen bees are bred on lonely Dartmoor at a permanent station not far from Dartmeet but the 300 or so hives from which the honey is produced are scattered around the grounds of the Abbey as well as on neighbouring farms. During late summer, however, these hives are taken on to Dartmoor where the bees can feast on the fragrant nectar of the heather blossom which gives the honey its distinctive flavour. Brother Adam has been awarded the OBE for his work in breeding the Buckfast Bee.

sions in the rocks which have been cut away by the animal grinding out a 'home base' on the rock. Below the water line, sea anemones wave their coloured tentacles in search of food; left high and dry, they contract into a blob of maroon jelly. Lift the stones in the pool and you will uncover small edible crabs, velvet swimming crabs, and the ubiquitous shore crab. (Remember to replace the stone as you found it; left exposed, the many creatures living on its underside will die.)

A walk along the shore can also be rewarding. Look for small shells with neat holes drilled in them; these have been attacked and eaten by the dog whelk. Here and there you will find the long and aptly named razor shells, or a piece of cuttle bone, or a mermaid's purse — the egg sac of a dogfish or a ray.

The sea

Hidden from the gaze of all but the snorkeller of the scuba diver, the wealth of life beneath the sea almost defies description. The waters of Devon's south coast are rich in marine life, from the tiniest of plankton to the vast basking shark which can grow up to 40 feet long and weigh as much as 7 tons. Despite their size, they are plankton feeders, filtering up to 330 000 gallons of water every hour. Between these two extremes, a vast array of fishes and crustaceans has traditionally provided a rich harvest for the Devon fishermen, while the clear warm waters encourage the growth of an abundance of corals, such as the fan coral which grows at a rate of less than half an inch a year.

Undoubtedly, the most prolific fish is the mackerel, though numbers have declined alarmingly in recent years. Huge shoals swim close offshore in mid-water, snatching at everything that passes — which makes them a very easy fish to catch on a hook baited with almost anything. Around the rocks and reefs can be found pollack and various species of multi-coloured wrasse, many of which begin life as females and then, as they age, change their sex to become males. On the sandy bottom, flattened by evolution and coloured on their topside like the sand on which they live, are the various species of flatfishes, such as plaice, turbot, and brill. The Skerries Bank, in Start Bay, is justly famous for its fishing for these species, because it provides a very important breeding habitat for them.

The lobster has been in decline for some time, mainly through overfishing, but the edible crab is caught in larger numbers around Devon than anywhere else along the English coast, with no sign of this diminishing its numbers,

Only above the sea can evidence of all this richness be found. A school of dolphins may break the surface as they pursue the mackerel shoals; a seal's head may be seen among the beds of kelp. But, most of all, there are the birds: gulls and terns, guillemots and razorbills, battalions of cormorants resting on rocks before setting off for another fishing trip. All of these animals, situated at the top of the marine food chain, bear witness to the wealth of life beneath the waters of Devon's south coast.

In no other area is this wealth better known than along a stretch of coast to the east of Plymouth ★ . The Wembury ★ Voluntary Marine Conservation Area runs from Plymouth Sound to the mouth of the Yealm and includes both the seashore and offshore waters. The area has strata of soft rock in which innumerable nooks, crannies, and gullies have been carved by the sea. This makes it very rich in marine life, and it has been extensively studied over the years — it is still heavily used for field trips. This, and the pressure of visitors to the beach, began to threaten the wildlife of the area, and a Marine Conservation Area was established. Guided walks and rockpool rambles are on offer during the summer months organized by the Devon Wildlife Trust's Marine Conservation staff, who have a special responsibility for the area.

All in all, South Devon and Dartmoor have at least as much to offer to the committed naturalist as to the average holidaymaker. From the high, rocky tors to the flower-rich banks of the sunken lanes; from ancient woodlands to spectacular coast, there is something here for anyone who is looking for a holiday on the wild side but who might also want a comfortable hotel or lively nightlife.

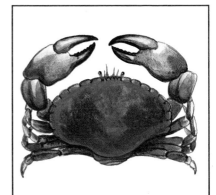

Small edible crabs are often found under stones in rock pools.

Leisure Activities

Useful Names and Addresses

TRANSPORT
Motoring

Automobile Association. The AA has a national Freefone number: (0800) 887766. All calls on this number are automatically redirected via British Telecom to the area number in which the call is being made; also Exeter (0392) 32121; Plymouth (0752) 669989 . Royal Automobile Club. Exeter (0392) 58333; Plymouth Tel. (0752) 669301.

Bus, Coach etc

Bayline Mini Bus Hire (0803) 525555. Burtons Coaches (08045) 2106/6106. Dartmouth Motors (08043) 2134/5. Devon General Limited: (0392) 56231. Garretts of Devon (0626) 66580. W Hard & Son (03647) 3227. Knightline Coaches of Torquay (0803) 37600. Millmans Coaches (0364) 42307. National Bus Company: Exeter (0392) 215454; Plymouth (0752) 671121. Plymouth Citybus (0752) 264888/668000. Silverline Coaches (0803) 558136. H & A Sleep, Bere Alston (0822) 840244. Snell Coaches (0626) 2080. Sticklepath Garage (0837) 840601. Southern National Limited (0823) 72033. Tally Ho Coaches (0548) 3081. Torbay Riviera Coaches (0803) 313413. Torquay Travel Limited (0803) 212900. Ugborough Car Sales (0752) 894740. Wallace Arnold Coaches (0803) 552255. Western National Limited (0752) 664011. Western National and Devon General (0803) 63226. Keith Williams Tavel (0803) 34597. Yelloway Trathen Express Limited (0752) 790565.

Train

Talking Timetable: London-Plymouth (Mon-Fri trains) (0752) 666030, (Sat trains) (0752) 667117, (Sun trains) (0752) 667373; London-Newton Abbott (Mon-Fri trains) (0803) 213771, (Sat trains) (0803) 212626, (Sun trains) (0803) 213773.
Exeter (0392) 433551. Plymouth (0752) 221300. Torquay (0803) 25911.
Dart Valley Light Railway (0364) 42338 or (0803) 555872. Plym Valley Railway, Marsh Mills Station, Coypool Road, Marsh Mills, Plymouth.

Boat Trips and Cruises

Brixham Belle Pleasure Cruises, Brixham (08045) 2707. G H Ridalls & Sons (The Red Cruisers), Dartmouth (08043) 2109. Grand Western Horseboat Company, Tiverton (0884) 253345. Greenway — Dittisham Ferry & Boat Hire (0803) 844010 (summer), (080422) 264 (winter). River Link, Dartmouth (08043) 4488. Torbay Seaway, Torquay (0803) 214397.

Cycle Hire

Dartmoor Cycle Hire, North Tawton (083782) 685. Plymvale Mountain Bike Hire, Plymouth (0752) 340437.

Yacht and Boat Charter

The Boy David (0803) 558858. Brixham Self-drive Motor Boats (08045) 2046. Coral Star III Cruises (0803) 555115. Dart Pleasure Craft Limited (08043) 4488. Devon Princess Cruises (0803) 26606. Devonshire Coast Cruises Trawler Yacht 'Regard' (0621) 76422. Distin & Bell (08043) 2534. Jib-Set Sail School (0803) 25414. Paignton Boat Co. (0803) 521683. L M Saunders (0803) 554341. Sparkle Pleasure Cruises (0803) 523948. Sunshine Cruises (0803) 27258. Torquay Speedboats (0803) 25445. M R Walker (08045) 55735. Western Lady Ferry Service (0803) 27292.

LEISURE ACTIVITIES
Angling

Information concerning fishing on reservoirs is available from Recreation Office, South West Water, Peninsula House, Rydon Lane Exeter EX2 7HR, Tel (0392) 219666 or from the Ranger of individual waters as follows: Meldon (06473) 2440; Burrator (0822) 853353; Venford (06473) 2440; Old Mill (08043) 3509; Squabmoor (0392) 219666; Fernworthy (06473) 2440; Kennick, Tottiford and Trenchford (06473) 2440.
Coarse Fishing
Contact local fishing tackle shops for permits for: Exe and Exeter Canal; Grand Western Canal, Tiverton; Newton Abbot Ponds; Stover Lake, Newton Abbot.
Slapton Ley (0548) 580466.
Game fishing
Deer Park Hotel, Honiton Tel (0404) 2064. Holne Chase Hotel, Ashburton Tel (03643) 471.
Permits are available from local hotels, inns, shops, tackle shops for certain waters on the following rivers: Dart, Teign, Tamar, Walkham, Plym, Meavy.
Coarses: Charles Bingham (Fishing) Limited, The Rod Room, Broad Park, Coryton, Nr Okehampton, Tel (082286) 281.
Sea Fishing
Unless otherwise given here, contact the appropriate local Tourist Information Centre.
Plymouth Angling Boatman's Association (0752) 221722. Sidmouth (03955) 4947. Teignmouth, J Ellyatt, 3 Interteign Drive. Also from Beesands.

Board Sailing

Meldon Reservoir, Nr Okehampton. Contact Meldon Sailing Club Secretary (0837) 82421. Plymouth (0752) 268328. Torquay (0803) 550180, (0803) 212411.

Camping and Caravanning
Camping and Caravanning in South Devon available from Torbay Tourist Board (0803) 296296,
'Camping and Caravanning Sites' information also included in *The Dartmoor Visitor* available from Dartmoor National Park Information Centres.

Canoeing
Canoeing is limited in the Dartmoor area because of the possible disturbance to winter spawning and to summer game fishing. Contact D Scrase on (0803) 812389 for further information about canoeing on certain sections of the River Dart.

Cricket
Sidmouth Cricket, Lawn Tennis, and Croquet Club (03955) 3229.

Cycling
'Plym Valley Cycle Track' information available from Tourist Information Centre, Plymouth.

Diving
Torcross Underwater Diving Centre, contact D Light, Hallsands Hotel, North Hallsands.

Golf
Axe Cliff Golf Club, Axmouth (0297) 20499. Bigbury-on-Sea (0548) 810557. Churston Down Road, Tavistock (0822) 2344. Churston Golf Club (0803) 842218. Crediton (03632) 3025. Dawlish Warren Golf Club (0626) 862255. Elfordleigh Golf Club, Plympton (0752) 336428. Exeter (039287) 4139. Honiton Golf Club (0404) 2943/44422. Manor House Hotel, Nr Moretonhampstead (0647) 40355. Sidmouth Golf Club (03955) 3451. Staddon Heights Golf Club, Plymouth (0752) 492630. Stover (0626) 52460. Teignmouth (06267) 4194. Thurlestone (0548) 560405. Torquay (St Marychurch) (0803) 37471. Tors Road, Nr Okehampton (0837) 2113. Wrangaton (03647) 3229. Yelverton Golf Club (0822) 852824.

Greyhound Racing
Exeter (0392) 73132.

Hang Gliding
Devon School of Hang Gliding (0752) 564408. South Devon Hang Gliding Club (0752) 709987.
Note that it is an offence to take off or to land on any of the Dartmoor Commons

without proper consent and that hang gliding must never be undertaken anywhere without the permission of the land-owner.

Horse Racing
Haldon Racecourse, Exeter (0392) 832599. Newton Abbot Racecourse (0626) 3235.

Leisure Centres
Exeter (0392) 221771. Seaton (0297) 20932. Torquay, English Riviera Centre (0803) 299992.

Para-Gliding
Torquay (0803) 559769, (0803) 295445.

Riding
Abigail Equestrian Centre, Chudleigh (0626) 852167. Babeny Farm Riding Stables, Poundsgate (03643) 296. Barton Riding and Livery Stable, Torquay (0803) 35233. Blackslade Riding Centre, Widecombe-in-the-Moor (03642) 304. California Riding School, California Cross (0548) 566. Cheston Farm Equestrian Centre, Wrangaton (03647) 3266. Cholwell Farm & Riding Stables, Mary Tavy (082281) 526. Court Barton Timeshare, Kingsbridge (0548) 561919/561240. Devenish Pitt Tables, Farway (040487) 355. Eastlake Stables, Belstone (0837) 52513. Elliots Hill Riding Centre, Buckland-in-the-Moor, (0364) 53058. Felgwyn Stud Riding School, Kingsbridge (0548) 3009/53561. Goodmores Riding School and Trekking Centre, Exmouth (0395) 264115. Great Sherberton Stables, Hexworthy (03643) 276. Haldon Lodge Riding Stables, Kennford (0392) 68683. Higher Bowden Riding Centre (0626) 833353. Hillside Riding Centre, Merrivale (082289) 458. Lydford House Riding Stables (082282) 347. Moorland Riding Stables, Peter Tavy (082281) 293. Myrtle Farm Riding Stables, Axminster (0460) 20442. Pinhoe Riding Centre (0392) 68683. Primley Riding Stables, Paignton (0803) 557222. Shilstone Rocks Riding & Trekking Centre (03642) 281. Skaigh Stables (0837) 840429. Smallacombe Farm Riding Stables, Ilsington (03646) 265. Two Bridges Hotel (02289) 206. Two Bridges Riding Stable (082289) 287. George Westaway & Son, Totnes (0803) 863023. Wembury Bay Riding School (0752) 862676.

Roller Skating
Plymouth (0752) 220077.

Sailing
Brixham Marina (0803) 882929. Brixham Yacht Club (08045) 3332. Mayflower Marina, Plymouth (0752) 556633. Newton Ferrers Sailing School (0752) 872375. Ply-

mouth Sailing School (0752) 667170. Port of Plymouth Sailing Association (0752) 773430. Queen Anne' Battery Seasports Centre, Plymouth (0752) 671142. Royal Plymouth Corinthian Yacht Club (0752) 664327. Royal Torbay Yacht Club (0803) 292006. Royal Western Yacht Club, Plymouth (0752) 660077. Salcombe Yacht Club (054884) 2445. Sidmouth Sailing Club (03955) 5116. Torquay Marina (0803) 214624. Torquay Yacht Harbours (0803) 213721.

Speedway
Exeter (0647) 52046.

Sports Centres
Exeter (0392) 217966. Exmouth (0395) 266381. Honiton (0404) 2325. Kingsbridge (0548) 7100. Newton Abbot (0626) 60426. Ottery St Mary (040481) 2310. Plymouth (0752) 702492, (0752) 564112. Teignmouth (06267) 5940. Torquay (0803) 38819, (0803) 52240.

Squash
Clennon Valley, Paignton (0803) 521990. Exeter (0392) 36100. Plymouth (0752) 777454. Torquay (0803) 33491, (0803) 211161, (0803) 24301, (0803) 22271, (0803) 24361.

Stock Car Racing
Newton Abbot (on the Racecourse) (0626) 2627.

Swimming Pools
Bovey Tracey (0626) 832828. Brixham (08045) 7151. Chagford (06473) 3378. Dawlish (0626) 864394. Exeter (0392) 54489. Exmouth (0395) 266381. Honiton (0404) 3228. Newton Abbot (0626) 5118 and (0626) 67544. Okehampton (0837) 2073. Paignton (0803) 521990. Plymouth (0752) 264894/264895/264896, (0752) 663665, (0752) 664644. Salcombe (054884) 2155. Tavistock (0822) 4350. Teignmouth (06267) 6271 (ext. 243). Topsham (039287) 4477. Totnes (0803) 863848. Torquay (0803) 212525, (0803) 33400.

Tennis
Brixham (08045) 477. Dawlish (0626) 863589/865746. Exeter (0392) 77888 (ext. 2447). Honiton (0404) 2325. Kingsbridge (0548) 3039. Okehampton (0837) 2073. Plymouth (0752) 264840. Salcombe (054884) 2794. Teignmouth (06267) 6271 (ext. 259). Torquay (0803) 22786, (0803) 23752.

Walks
Information on Guided Walks is available from the Dartmoor National Park Informa-

tion Centres or from the Dartmoor National Park Authority's free newspaper, *The Dartmoor Visitor*. Dartmoor National Park Authority publishes a series of 'Walks Around' leaflets which are also available from Information Centres. Information from (0626) 832093.

There is a South Devon Heritage Coast collection of coast path guides available from Assistant Heritage Coast Officer, Follaton House, Plymouth Road, Totnes, Devon TQ9 5NE, Tel (0803) 864499.

Information on the South West Peninsula Coast Path available from Eric Wallis, Secretary, South West Way Association, 'Windlestraw', Penquit, Ermington, Nr Ivybridge, Devon Tel (0752) 896237. The National Trust also publishes a series of 'Map and Guide' leaflets to those stretches of the coast path owned by the Trust. The series is available from National Trust shops or by contacting The Information Officer, The National Trust, Killerton House, Broadclyst, Exeter EX5 3LE, Tel (0392) 881691.

Other literature on walking may be obtained by sending an SAE to the following organizations:

Countryside Commission Publications Despatch, 19-23 Albert Road, Manchester MI9 2EQ.

Field Studies Council, Slapton Ley Field Centre, Slapton, Kingsbridge, Devon, TQ7 2QP

Forestry Commission, 231 Corstorphine Road, Edinburgh EH12 7AT.

Long Distance Walkers Association, 29 Appledown Close, Alresford, Hampshire SO24 9ND.

Ramblers' Association, 1-5 Wandsworth Road, London SW8 2LJ.

Water Skiing
Torquay (0803) 295445, (0803) 559769.

Youth Hostels
Some hostels are not open during the winter. Contact YHA Area Office.

YHA Area Office, Belmont Place, Devonport Road, Stoke, Plymouth PL3 4DW Tel. (0752) 562753.

Beer (0297) 20296. Bellever (0822) 88227. Bigbury-on-Sea (0548) 810283. Dartington (0803) 862303. Exeter (Topsham) (039287) 3329. Gidleigh (06473) 2421. Plymouth (0752) 562189. Salcombe (054884) 2856. Start Bay (0803) 770013. Steps Bridge (0647) 52435.

PLACES TO VISIT

Abbeys, Minsters, and Priories
Buckfast Abbey (0364) 42761. Torre Abbey (0803) 23593.

Historic Houses, Castles, and Gardens,
Buckfast Butterflies (0364) 42916. Ugbrooke (0626) 852179.
Dartington Hall (0803) 862224. Dartmouth Castle (08043) 3588.
The Mansion House (08043) 2272. Mearsdon Manor (0647) 40483. Bradley Manor (0626) 4513. Compton Castle (08047) 2112. Kirkham House (0803) 522775. Oldway Mansion (0803) 550711. Paignton Zoological and Botanical Gardens (0803) 557479/527936. Bowden House (0803) 863664. Totnes Castle (0803) 864406. Totnes Guildhall (0803) 862147. Church House, Widecombe (03642) 321.

Country Parks and Farms
The River Dart Country Park Ltd (0364) 52511. Parke (0626) 832093). Parke Rare Breeds Farm (0626) 833909). Silverlands (06267) 2187. Dartmoor Wildlife Park (075537) 209. Powderham Castle (0626) 890243. Valley Springs Trout Farm (0548853) 574.

Mills, Breweries, Factories, and Craft Centres
Aidee Devon Violet Factory (0626) 833081. The Wheel - Craft Workshops. (0626) 852698. Dartington Cider Press Centre (0803) 864171. Loddiswell Vineyard (0548) 550221. House of Marbles and Teign Valley Glass Studios (06267) 3534. Babbacombe Pottery (0803) 38757. Moorland Craft Centre, Haytor (03646) 479. Lotus Pottery (080 428) 303. Woodturners Craft Centre (0548) 830405. Townstal Pottery (080 43) 2563.

Museums, Art Galleries, and Exhibitions
Ashburton Museum (0364) 53278. Devon Guild of Craftsmen (0626) 832223. British Fisheries Museum (08045) 2861. Brixham Marine, Aquarium and Trawling Exhibition (08045) 2204. Brixham Musuem (08045) 3203. Golden Hind (08045) 6223. Dartmouth Town Museum (08043) 2923. Henley Museum (08043) 2281. Newcomen Engine House (08043) 2923. Dawlish Museum (0626) 863318. Cookworthy Museum of Rural Life in South Devon (0548) 3235. Paignton Seashore Aquarium (0803) 522913. Torbay Trains, Robes, Roses, and Aircraft Museum (0803) 553540. Overbecks Museum and Garden (054884) 2893. Teignmouth Museum (06267) 4084. Shaldon Wildlife Trust (062687) 2234. Aqualand (0803) 24439. Model Village, Babbacombe (0803) 38669. Silvers Model World (0803) 23643. Torquay Museum (0803) 23975. Devonshire Collection of Period Costume (0803) 862423. Totnes Motor Museum (0803) 862777. The Totnes (Elizabethan) Museum (0803) 863821. The British Photographic Museum (0803) 863664. New World Tapestry (0803) 862020.

Natural Attractions
Becky Falls Estate (064 722) 259. Canonteign Falls and Farm Park (0647) 52666. Dartington Trails (0803) 864171. Dawlish Warren Nature Reserve (0626) 66951. Kent's Cavern Caves (0803) 24059. Yarner Wood Nature Reserve (0626) 832330.

Preserved Steam Railways
Dart Valley Steam Railway and Leisure Park (0364) 42338. The Brunel Atmospheric Railway (0626) 890000. Kingsbridge Miniature Railway (062 682) 361. Gorse Blossom Miniature Railway Park and Gardens (062 682) 361. Torbay and Dartmouth Railway (0803) 555872. The Cliff Railway (0803) 38750.

Dartmoor Information Centres
Postbridge Visitor Centre (0822) 88272. Princetown (082289) 414. Tavistock (0822) 612938. Steps Bridge (0647) 52018. Newbridge (03643) 303. Okehampton (0837) 3020. Parke Barn (0626) 832093.

Tourist Information Centres
Devon Tourist Information Centre, Exeter (0392) 437581/79088.
Axminster (0297) 34386. Bovey Tracey (0626) 832047. Brixham (08045) 2861. Budleigh Salterton (03954) 5275. Dartmouth (08043) 4224. Dawlish (0626) 863589. Exeter (0392) 265297/265700. Exmouth (0395) 263744. Honiton (0404) 3716. Ivybridge (0752) 897035. Kingsbridge (0548) 3195. Modbury (0548) 830159. Newton Abbot (0626) 67494. Okehampton (0837) 3020. Ottery St Mary (040481) 3964. Paignton (0803) 558383. Plymouth (0752) 264849/264851 and (0752) 223806. Salcombe (054884) 2736. Seaton (0297) 21660. Sidmouth (03955) 6441. Tavistock (0822) 2938. Teignmouth (06267) 79769. Torquay (0803) 27428. Totnes (0803) 863168.
Note that there are also more than 40 Information Boards in addition to the Centres.

Information

All National Park Information Services may be identified by this symbol — look out for it when travelling through the Dartmoor area.

Useful Telephone Numbers
Council for National Parks 071 240 3603/4.
Dartmoor Preservation Association, Secretary (0822) 853928. Devon Tourism (0392) 273260. Devon Wildlife Trust (0392) 79244. Firing Information Services (0803) 294592; (0392) 70164; (0752) 701924; (0837) 2939. South Hams Tourism (0803) 866425/ 864499. Teignbridge Services (0626) 61101. Torbay Tourist Board (0803) 296296. West Country Tourist Board (0392) 76351. West Devon Borough Council (0822) 5911 or (0837) 2901.

Further Useful Information

Market Days
MONDAY-SATURDAY Exeter, Exmouth, Honiton, Newton Abbot, Plymouth. MONDAY Plympton. TUESDAY Ash-burton, Dartmouth, Kingsbridge, Tavistock, Tiverton, Totnes. WEDNESDAY Tavistock. THURSDAY Axminster. FRIDAY Dartmouth, Tavistock, Tiverton, Totnes. SATURDAY Okehampton, Topsham.

EMERGENCY INFORMATION

Coastguards
Brixham Maritime Rescue Co-ordination Centre (08045) 58292. Hope Cove (0548) 561229. Prawle Point (054851) 259. Plymouth (0752) 670039.

Life Saving
Bantham Surf Life Saving Club (0548) 2605.

Widecombe in the Moor.

Places of Interest

Stars (★) after a place name indicate that the place is featured elsewhere in this section.

Abbots' Way
This is the modern name given to a route linking the abbeys of Buckfast ★ and Tavistock ★ . The monks of these abbeys, together with those at Buckland, grazed their sheep on the high moor and became wealthy and influential on the proceeds of the wool industry, exporting their cloth as far afield as Florence in Italy. The sheep drovers' routes on the moor were marked with granite crosses, some of which can still be seen today. The original route ran from Cross Furzes near Buckfast Abbey to Tavistock, dividing at Broad Rock with the 'branch line' going to Buckland Abbey. It is still possible to walk the route today although anyone doing so should be able to use a map and compass because many of the original stone markers have long since disappeared.

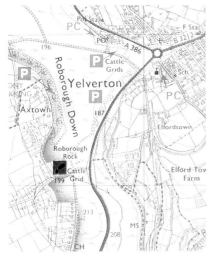

Aish Tor see New Bridge

À la Ronde
(192) (SY 0083) 1 mile N of Exmouth
À la Ronde or The Round House is an eighteenth-century, sixteen-sided house designed in 1795 by Jane and Mary Parminter and it remains in the ownership of the Parminter family still. It is said to be a combination of the styles of a 'rustic cottage' and a sixth-century Byzantine basilica from Italy. By any standards it is an oddity, especially somehow because it is still occupied. À la Ronde may be visited from **Tour 1**.

Ashburton
(202) (SX 7670) 3 miles NE of Buckfastleigh
Ashburton lies close by the new A38 trunk road, in wooded country on the edge of the south-

eastern boundary of Dartmoor on a tributary of the River Dart. Despite its population of little more than 2000 people, it is still a busy town and is important historically as one of Devon's four most important stannary, or tin-producing, towns which it became in 1305. Ashburton is recorded in the Domesday Book in 1086 as belonging to the Bishop of Exeter and, in addition to coigning tin, it has been a centre for Devon's cloth trade as well as for manufacturing pewter, paints and dyes, and for producing a local limestone known as Ashburton Marble. It boasts a number of important buildings, not least of which is the medieval Chapel of St Lawrence, parts of which date back to the thirteenth century. In 1983, the Dartmoor National Park Authority took over the responsibility for this building and, with a grant from English Heritage, it has fully restored this historic building. In its time, the Chapel has been a chantry chapel, a grammar school, and a meeting place for the ancient Courts of Leet and Baron. There are other slate-roofed, gable-styled, Elizabethan, Georgian, and Victorian buildings to be seen in the main streets, and the local museum in West Street is worth a visit.

About 3 miles west of Ashburton is The River Dart Country Park. In a lovely riverside estate, there are adventure playgrounds, bathing in a river-fed lake, picnic meadows, woodland walks, pony riding, and the so-called 'Anaconda Run'. If you bring your own rods, there is even salmon and trout fishing available. Ashburton is an ideal place from which to explore Dartmoor and is on **Tour 4**.

Ashprington
(202) (SX 8157) 3 miles S of Totnes
Situated in a peninsula-like triangle of high ground between the River Dart and Bow Creek leading from the Harbourne River, in one of the most attractive parts of the South Hams District, Ashprington is a lovely old village. Its fifteenth-century church has a chalice which has been used continuously since the last quarter of the thirteenth century. On **Tour 6**.

Axminster
(193) (SY 2998)
Today, Axminster is a comparatively quiet town although the market is lively. It gets its name from its location on the River Axe and from the old abbey church or minster. It lies at the point where the Roman Fosseway crosses the ancient Icknield Street and there are many earthworks to be seen in the area. Few people throughout the world will not have heard the name 'Axminster' even if they have never been within a thousand miles of the town. Axminster has been famous for its carpets since 1755 when the first one was woven by Thomas Whitty although, between 1835 and 1936, manufacture ceased. It is worth paying a visit to Axminster Carpets, near the station off King Edward Road, at any time of the year to watch carpets being made. The museum housed in The Old Courthouse in Church Street also has a special display on the history of carpet making.

Just off the A35, a little to the west of the town

is the village of Shute with the remains of the Shute Barton Manor House. This was completed in the sixteenth century and has a remarkable gatehouse as well as a tower with battlements and some interesting late Gothic windows. Shute Barton is owned by the National Trust and is open on certain days of the week from April to October. Axminster is the starting point for **Tour 1**.

Babbacombe Model Village see Torquay

Becky Falls
(191) (SX 7680) 1 mile SE of Manaton
Becky, or Becka Falls, is a 70-foot waterfall on the Becka Brook, a tributary of the River Bovey. The falls are situated among lovely woodlands in a privately owned estate and are well worth a visit. There is a newly renovated café and gift

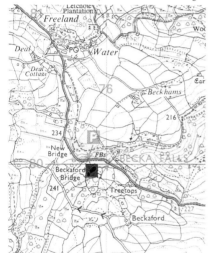

shop, and the estate owners have planned out several interesting nature trails as well as publishing an excellent *Spotter Book* and informative *Souvenir Guide*. Becky Falls can be visited from **Tour 4**.

Beer
(192) (SY 2289) 1 mile W of Seaton
Despite its proximity to Seaton ★ , a larger holiday resort, Beer has managed to retain its charm and authenticity as a fishing village (it was once a favourite haunt of smugglers, too!). The little bay is delightful and you can buy fresh fish there, as well as watching the fishermen use the old capstans to haul their boats up the beach. The extensive underground caverns of Beer Quarry Caves in Quarry Lane were first dug by the Romans for building stone and were in constant use for almost 2000 years. It is well worth taking one of the guided tours. The Peco-

Situated among lovely woodlands, Becky Falls (left) are well worth a visit. Once a favourite haunt of smugglers, Beer (above) remains a delightful fishing village.

rama Pleasure Park is a favourite with children but there are also lovely gardens. Beer is on **Tour 1** and **Walk 1** also begins from Beer Head.

Bellever Forest
(191) (SX 6577) 1½ miles SE of Postbridge
Bellever Forest was planted with coniferous trees by the Duchy of Cornwall in the 1920s for quick-maturing timber production. It is now Forestry Commission land and there are walks set out in the forest — a guide book is available from the car park. **Tour 4** takes you past Bellever Forest.

Belstone
(191) (SX 6193) 2 miles SE of Okehampton
Situated so close to the busy town of Okehampton ★ and the new A30 bypass, it is remarkable what an untouched, quiet, little stone-built vil-

The village of Belstone on the edge of Dartmoor.

lage Belstone is. It lies close the River Taw, which eventually finds its way to the sea at Barnstaple in North Devon, and is right on the edge of Dartmoor to which it offers good access. In the centre of the village are stocks constructed from wood and stone. Belstone is on **Tour 8**.

Bere Alston

(201) (SX 4466) 6 miles NW of Plymouth
Although Bere Ferrers ★ is the parish, Bere Alston, closer to the River Tamar, has become

Once a busy commercial quay, Weir Quay at Bere Alston is now given over to leisure sailing.

the larger of the villages. It is no longer a mining village, but its associations with mining date from the thirteenth century. Weir Quay on the River Tamar was once a busy commercial quay but now it is given over to leisure sailing, and is well worth a visit for a relaxing stroll around. **Tour 10** passes through Bere Alston.

Bere Ferrers

(201) (SX 4563) 2 miles S of Bere Alston
Lying on the banks of the River Tavy and in the peninsula-like stretch of land between the Tavy and the Tamar to the west, the village of Bere Ferrers has a most interesting parish church in which a good deal of the fourteenth-century structure still remains.

Berry Head

(202) (SX 9456) 1 mile NE of Brixham
Berry Head forms one of the tips of the pincers of land surrounding Torbay. The lighthouse at Berry Head is often described as the 'shortest and the highest' in Britain since it is only 12 feet high but stands on a 200-foot cliff. Many of the cliff-nesting seabirds, such as kittiwakes and fulmars, can be seen here and, especially in spring, birdwatchers can have fine views of these and others as they soar around the cliffs. Berry Head Country Park is famous for its rare plants, too, growing on the limestone rocks. The huge fort, built to guard the coast against possible invasion by Napoleon, has erased the original Saxon fortification on this spot.

Berry Pomeroy Castle

(202) (SX 8361) 4 miles NW of Totnes
The castle ruins, in the Duke of Somerset's wooded estate of Berry Pomeroy, are reputed to be the most haunted in England. The fourteenth-century gatehouse, commanding the strong southern walls, is probably the oldest part of the castle. Within the castle walls, there is the ruin of a sixteenth-century mansion built by the Seymour family. The castle is privately owned but open to the public throughout the year.

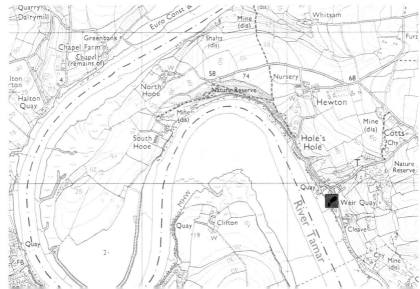

Bickleigh Castle
(192) (SS 9306) 9 miles N of Exeter

Bickleigh Castle is situated on the west bank of the River Exe and was once the home of the Earls of Devon. The three-story gatehouse with its great hall is the most complete remaining part of the orginal castle. The detached Chapel is Norman and dates from the eleventh century. Other features of interest include the armoury, guardroom, Tudor-style bedroom, and seventeenth-century farmhouse. There is an interesting museum of Victoriana as well as a collection of World War II spy and escape paraphernalia. Visits must be pre-booked and, except during the Easter and school summer holidays, all tours of the buildings are guided.

Bickleigh Mill
(192) (SS 9307) 10 miles N of Exeter

There has been a corn mill here, where the Rivers Dart and Exe meet, since the time of Domesday although the present building may be no older than early nineteenth century. The mill fell into disuse in the 1950s and continued to deteriorate until it was restored and reopened, this time as a craft centre, in 1976. The narrow bridge which crosses the Exe was supposed to have been the inspiration for Simon and Garfunkel's well-known song, *Bridge over Troubled Water* but it is also reputed to be haunted by a knight who lost his head (literally) when denying right of way across the bridge to another traveller! Visitors to Devonshire's Centre at Bickleigh Mill can look at the working water mill and workshops, fish for trout using equipment on hire at the Centre, or wander around Birdland and the picnic centre. It is even possible to travel back in time more than 100 years in the nineteenth-century working farm where muscle power of horse and man are substituted for tractor and combine harvester; you can even

Top: *the beautiful coast near Bigbury-on-Sea.*
Above: *the ruins of Berry Pomeroy Castle, reputed to be the most haunted in England.*

try your hand at milking! Native otters are now rare in Devon but, at the Centre, you can see the closely related short-clawed otters which are kept here.

Bicton Park see Budleigh Salterton

Bigbury-on-Sea
(202) (SX 6444) 6 miles W of Kingsbridge

The little seaside resort of Bigbury-on-Sea offers cafés, shops, and a pleasant stretch of sands. The beach faces, and is separated from, Burgh Island by a tidal causeway, or tombola, which, at low tide, can be crossed on foot. At high tide, however, it is still possible to reach the island when the odd-looking sea tractor is running. From Bigbury, the fourteenth-century Pilchard Inn, notorious for smuggling, on Burgh Island is clearly visible. At the highest point of the island stand the ruins of a small stone house which is thought to have been built for picnic parties in the nineteenth century. Bigbury is also the start of **Walk 6**.

Blackpool Sands
(202) (SX 8547) 3 miles SW of Dartmouth
Just by the A379 road, Blackpool Sands is a pleasant, privately owned beach with adequate facilities and windsurfing. Its south-east-facing aspect and sheltered position make a favourite sunspot. On **Tour 6**.

Bovey Tracey
(191) (SX 8178) 5 miles NW of Newton Abbot
Located on the edge of Dartmoor by the River Bovey — pronounced 'Buvvy' — the second part of the name derives from the twelfth-century knight, William Tracey who acquired the town. It is believed that, in 1170, Sir William took part in the murder of Thomas à Becket, the Archbishop of Canterbury who opposed the policies of Henry II. He then repented of his crime, built what is now the parish church, and dedicated it to St Thomas. Bovey Tracey is an attractive, workaday place seeming to be less of a dormitory town than some of its neighbours. The lower end of Bovey is dominated by the methodist church while, up the hill, the Council Chambers and Town Hall, with its double red doors, looks for all the world like a fire station. The old stone and slate Riverside Mill, with its restored undershot wheel, now houses the exhibition gallery, sales area, and café of The Devon Guild of Craftsmen. On the Newton Road, it is possible to visit the Aidee Devon Violet Factory and watch the well-known local perfume being made. Bovey Tracey is an ideal centre from which to explore eastern Dartmoor. About 2 miles to the west of Bovey is Yarner Wood National Nature Reserve managed by the Nature Conservancy Council. Here there is an educational nature trail as well as a woodland

The Dartmoor National Park Headquarters at Parke (top) and The Devon Guild Craft Centre, Bovey Tracey.

walk where visitors can look at the management work being carried out there. A short distance along the B3387 Haytor ★ / Widecombe ★ road is the Dartmoor National Park Headquarters and Rare Breeds Farm at Parke. Here there is an excellent Interpretation Centre as well as woodland and riverside strolls. Bovey Tracey is visited on **Tours 2** and **3**.

Bowden House
(202) (SX 8058) 1 mile S of Totnes
There was a dwelling on the site of the existing Bowden House as early as Roman times and a seventh-century gravestone was found here. The present house, with its elegant Queen Anne façades on the south-eastern and south-western approaches, dates largely from the early eighteenth century when it was rebuilt and enlarged by the new owner, Nicholas Trist. The house is currently owned by the Petersen family who can be contacted to arrange tours of the property. In the grounds of the house is the British Photographic Museum, an Aladdin's cave of cameras and other photographic paraphernalia. This was opened in June 1987 by Earl Shelburne in a building designed to blend well with its surroundings. Bowden House can be visited from **Tour 6**.

Bradley Manor see Newton Abbot

Branscombe
(192) (SY 1988) 3 miles W of Beer
An attractive, coastal village, Branscombe boasts a church with a Norman tower and three-decker pulpit, and a bakery with wood-burning ovens. There is still a traditional working smithy here housed in a lovely thatch-roofed building. The Sea Shanty Café at Branscombe Mouth was once a walled coal yard receiving coal direct

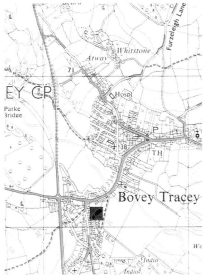

Bovey Tracey

from South Wales by boat. Until recently, pebbles from the beach were gathered on a commercial scale to use in the grinding processes of the cosmetics industry, and there was even a lime kiln and a gypsum mill here. Fishermen still go out from the Mouth. Much of the area is owned by the National Trust, and the West and East Cliffs as well as the beach are open to the public.

Brixham
(202) (SX 9355) 6 miles S of Torquay
Driving down into the narrow streets of Brixham on a weekday during the height of the holiday season may be a slow business, but it is worth the effort. The town is a fascinating fusion of holiday resort and working port where tiers of fishermen's cottages are punctuated by hotels and guest houses. Trawlers lie alongside pleasure boats in the busy harbour, and it is possible to find boats to take you around Torbay or the Dart estuary. There is a full-scale replica of *The Golden Hind*, Sir Francis Drake's ship, in the inner harbour and this is open to the public. There are collections of clothing of the period as well as jewellery and weapons. Pay a visit to the Old Market House by the harbour. As well as the tourist information centre, which will provide you with town trails, there is an excellent fisheries museum.

Brixham Museum at Bolton Cross includes the National Coastguard Museum. The new marina, Prince William Quay, marks the town's continuing connexion with the Netherlands, for it was at Brixham in 1688 that William of Orange stepped ashore to take the throne of England. **Tour 6** passes through Brixham.

The Brunel Atmospheric Pumping House at Starcross.

Brunel Atmospheric Pumping House
(192) (SX 9781) Starcross 2 miles N of Dawlish
The Pumping House was built in 1845 and, as well as housing a working atmospheric railway engine, there is an exhibition and an audiovisual show. Isambard Kingdom Brunel developed a design for a railway which was first invented by Joseph and Jacob Samuda and Samuel Clegg. The idea was simple. Between the rails of the track was a pipe connected to the rolling stock via a piston and an arm. Along the line, there were pumping houses in which steam engines could be used to create a partial vacuum in the pipe in front of the train. In this way, it was therefore atmospheric pressure behind the train which provided the power. The trains could be lighter, because there was no need for a locomotive, and the track would last longer because there was less wear. For various design reasons, however, the system did not work to full efficiency even though some trains did achieve speeds of up to 70 miles an hour. The

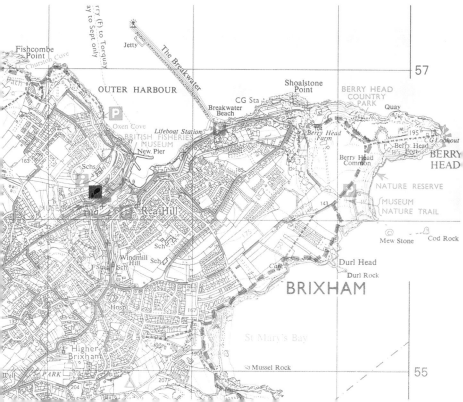

BUCKFAST ABBEY

line reverted to conventional locomotives after 1848. **Tour 3** passes the Pumping House.

Buckfast Abbey
(202) (SX 7467) 1 mile N of Buckfastleigh
Buckfast Abbey describes itself as a 'living Benedictine monastery' and, although its history goes back nearly 1000 years to 1018 when the first abbey was founded here, the present building was constructed on medieval foundations in 1882 by French Benedictine monks. The original monastery was destroyed in 1539 during Henry VIII's Dissolution. Parts of the medieval buildings, such as the Guest Hall, still remain and the monks are planning to restore it fully. Today, the Buckfast Abbey complex is a highly commercialised affair which it needs to be to sustain the abbey as new recruits to a monastic life become ever fewer. There are shops selling books, the Abbey's honey and tonic wine, and other gifts, as well as licensed tearooms and

The Dart Valley Light Railway at Buckfastleigh.

restaurant. There are even first-aid facilities and a baby-care centre — the monks seem to have thought of everything to make a trip to the abbey more enjoyable. Interestingly, there is also a modest little, white, pebble-dashed Methodist church here, too.

Close by is Buckfast Spinning Mill which is the yarn-spinning division of the Axminster ★ Carpet Company. There has been a textile mill on this site since the industrial revolution, and the water supply is used for processing as well as for power. Buckfast Abbey can be visited by making a short diversion from **Tour 4**.

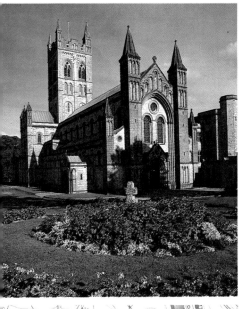

The 'living Benedictine monastery' of Buckfast Abbey.

Buckfastleigh
(202) (SX 7366) 6 miles NW of Totnes
Buckfastleigh is a small town, long associated with the wool trade, tucked among the wooded hills on the edge of the Dartmoor National Park. The limestone caverns of the Pengelley Cave Centre are well worth a visit. Close by is the well-known Buckfast Butterfly Farm where visitors can see butterflies from many parts of the world living and breeding in naturalistic habitat. Here, too, is the terminus for the Dart Valley Light Railway from where you can take a train, pulled by a carefully restored steam locomotive, on a trip up and down the picturesque line to Totnes. This is also the site of the Buckfast Steam and Leisure Park with its miniature railway and cinema. Buckfastleigh is the starting point for **Tour 4**.

Buckland Abbey see Buckland Monachorum

Buckland Monachorum
(201) (SX 4868) 6 miles S of Tavistock
This is an attractive village to stroll around, with some lovely buildings, and there is a car park by the church of St Andrew. The first church to be built here would have been a wooden structure dedicated to a Celtic saint. This was probably replaced by a stone-built church in the fourteenth century, although the present building dates from the late fifteenth century so that it is typical in its Perpendicular architecture of most of Dartmoor's churches. The font may be early Norman or even Saxon in origin. In 1581 Sir Francis Drake bought the nearby Buckland Abbey and would probably have visited Buckland Monachorum and its church.

Buckland Abbey was originally a Cistercian monastery and the building survived the Disso-

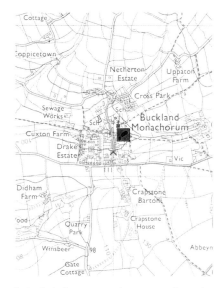

The pleasant, unspoiled little seaside resort gets its name from 'Budda's forest clearing' and from the Old English word meaning a 'saltworks' which refers to the saltpans which were once worked at the mouth of the River Otter. Budleigh Salterton has not changed very much since it began to attract its first tourists early in the nineteenth century. From the 500-foot, red sandstone cliffs behind the pebble beach there are good views into the next county and Lyme Bay. The Fairlynch Arts Centre and Museum housed in an eighteenth-century thatched house has an interesting display of costumes, local history and geology, natural history, and more.

The beach at Budleigh Salterton (below) *and Otterton Mill* (bottom), *found two miles to the north-east.*

lution by being converted to a country house by Sir Richard Grenville. It is owned now by the National Trust and houses a museum as well as 'Drake's Drum'. Buckland Abbey is open every day from April to October and on selected days for the rest of the year. Buckland Monachorum is passed on **Tour 10**.

Buckland-in-the-Moor
(191) (SX 7273) 6 miles E of Two Bridges
Despite having a population of less than 100 people, Buckland-in-the-Moor has been said to be one of England's most photographed villages — hardly surprising when you look at the picture-postcard thatched granite cottages between the little church of St Peter and the excellent viewpoint of Buckland Beacon. The clock on the church tower does not have the usual numerals but has letters spelling out the phrase 'MY DEAR MOTHER'. A short diversion from **Tour 4** will take you to Buckland.

Budleigh Salterton
(192) (SY 0681) 3 miles E of Exmouth

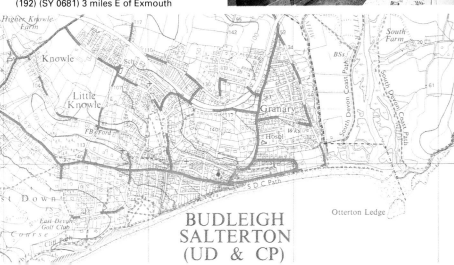

Two miles to the north-east, there is the Otterton Mill still powered by the River Otter and grinding wholemeal flour between its two fine millstones. It is now a mill centre and museum with art and craft gallery, craft shop, restaurant, bakery, and workshops. And 2 miles to the north of Budleigh, just to the west of the A376 road, are the 50 acres of Bicton Park with its bird garden, tropical house, gardens and entertainments for children. Budleigh Salterton is visited on **Tour 1**.

Burrator Reservoir
(202) (SX 5568) 3 miles E of Yelverton
Fed by the River Meavy, the 150-acre Burrator Reservoir was the first of several reservoirs to be built on Dartmoor to meet the ever-increasing demands for water from Plymouth and other South Devon towns and cities. It was originally constructed in 1898 but, as a plaque on the dam reveals, it was enlarged in 1928. A road circumnavigates the lake which remains perhaps the most attractive of all the moor's reservoirs. It is visited on **Tour 10**, and the area can be viewed from **Walk 12**.

Burrator Reservoir (below) *and Ditsworthy Warren* (bottom), *viewed from* **Walk 12**.

Canonteign Falls.

Cadhay Manor see Ottery St Mary

Canonteign Falls
(191) (SX 8382) 3 miles NW of Chudleigh
Opened to the public in 1985, Canonteign Falls and Country Park is set among some spectacularly beautiful, privately owned woodland and farmland in the Teign valley. The gorge was landscaped more than a century and a half ago by the first Viscountess Exmouth but was then allowed to fall into disuse. As well as claiming the highest waterfall in England, there are other falls, and ornamental lakes, as well as various tourist attractions such as the Bonehill Collection of Farm Machinery.

Castle Drogo

(191) (SX 7290) 3 miles NE of Chagford
Situated on a high, 900-foot promontory overlooking the Teign Valley, Castle Drogo has been described as 'the last great country house to be built in Britain'. Despite its medieval appearance, the castle was designed in this century by Sir Edwin Lutyens and not completed until 1930, only a year before the death of its owner, Julius Drewe, who had made his fortune from the chain of Home and Colonial grocery stores. Drewe was brought to the area because he thought his family may have been linked to that of the Norman Dru de Teigne whose name is also reflected in that of nearby Drewsteignton. Castle Drogo boasted its own hydro-electric system to provide power and even had an internal telephone system. Drogo was an alternative spelling for Dru. Although a descendant of Drewe still lives in the castle, it is now owned by the National Trust and is open to the public from April until October. It is possible to hire equipment to play that most aristocratic of games, croquet, on the huge lawns here. You pass by Castle Drogo on **Tour 2**.

Chagford

(191) (SX 7087) 10 miles SE of Okehampton
No trip to Dartmoor would be complete without visiting the charming little stannary town of Chagford. The name was originally spelt 'Cagefort', a Saxon name meaning 'gorsey spot where the River Teign was forded'. Between its recording in Domesday and 1300, Chagford developed as a marketing centre for the neighbouring hill farmers although tin mining was also taking place in the area as early as 1105. In 1305 Chagford was listed in a tinners' charter as a coignage town, and there are the remains of mainly medieval tin workings all around. It is interesting to note that some of the farms in the area had not seen wheeled traffic as recently as the 1830s. From the mid-nineteenth century, however, Chagford began to open its doors to tourists and in the later half of the century, George Hayter planned a drainage system as well as inspiring the Gas Company to provide gas lighting for the streets and some of the houses in 1869. In 1891, electricity came to Chagford and the town became one of the first places west of London to have electric street lighting.

The famous Dartmoor guide, James Perrot, also lived in Chagford between 1854 and 1895 —

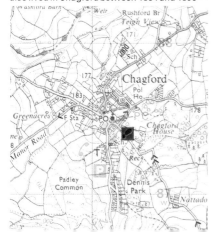

The charming little town of Chagford.

he is buried in the churchyard of St Michael's Church. The church was first dedicated in 1261 although the present building dates mainly from the fifteenth century. An oak tree once stood outside the southern wall of the churchyard and it has been suggested that the tree marked the spot where Christians first met to worship. Chagford is visited on **Tour 2** and passed on **Tour 8**.

Chudleigh

(191) (SX 8679) 10 miles SW of Exeter
Situated in the heart of the Teign valley and now bypassed by the A38 trunk road, Chudleigh is a pleasant town dating from the eleventh century. It was a medieval wool town but a large part of it was destroyed by fire in 1807. Old buildings and narrow lanes have survived, however, and Chudleigh is an excellent centre from which to explore Dartmoor and South Devon. The Wheel — Craft Workshops, housed in mill buildings in Clifford Street and with a working backshot water wheel, offer a variety of craft workshops and a restaurant.

A little to the south-west of the town centre is Silverlands all-weather attraction where there is an animated model circus, an enchanted forest, and craft workshops. Chudleigh Motor Museum, between Chudleigh and Chudleigh Knighton houses a unique collection of historic vehicles. Chudleigh is visited on **Tour 3**.

Cider Press Centre see Totnes

Clyst St Mary see **Tour 1**

The Half Moon pub at Clyst St Mary.

Cockington
(202) (SX 8963) 1 mile W of Torquay
Despite its proximity to the busy holiday resort of Torquay ★, the preserved thatched village of Cockington exudes old-world charm and has a history which dates back to before the Norman Conquest. It boasts a fourteenth-century forge and a sixteenth-century manor house set in almost 300 acres of lovely parkland. It was, in fact, a typical medieval village in which the villagers worked for, and were disciplined by, the Lord of the Manor. The oldest part of the existing Church of St George and St Mary is the tower which probably dates back to the thirteenth century although there was a church on this site 200 years earlier. The Drum Inn is actually a comparatively modern building designed by Sir Edwin Lutyens as a thatch-roofed and lime-washed structure to fit in with its surroundings. A leaflet available from the Torquay Tourist Information Centre in Vaughan Parade describes an excellent 2½ mile walk which takes in the village and Cockington Court. During the main holiday season, it is possible to take a ride in a horse-drawn landau. A short diversion from **Tour 5** will take you to Cockington.

Coleton Fishacre Garden
(202) (SX 9050) 1½ miles W of Kingswear
Owned by the National Trust, this is a lovely coastal garden set in woodland where there are superb sea views. There are many rare plants, shrubs, and trees, some of which are on sale. The possible short-cut from **Walk 3** passes through Coleton Fishacre.

Colyton
(192) (SY 2493) 2½ miles N of Seaton
Colyton has been a market town since Saxon times. Set in the valley of the River Coly, a tributary of the Axe, Colyton lays claim to be the

The lovely coastal garden of Coleton Fishacre.

'prettiest town in Devon'. The tannery in King Street, run by J and F J Baker and Co. is one of just two tanneries remaining in England where oak bark is used in the tanning process. It is open to the public throughout the year. Not far away is Farway Countryside Park where there is a rare breeds farm.

Compton Castle
(202) (SX 8664) 4 miles W of Torquay
Another property now run by the National Trust, Compton Castle is a fortified manor house built in three separate periods during the fourteenth, fifteenth, and sixteenth centuries by the Gilbert family who still have there home here. It is open to the public between April and October. **Tour 5** passes close to Compton Castle.

Cornwood
(202) (SX 6059) 3 miles NW of Ivybridge
Cornwood is a picturesque village which lies just inside the National Park boundary in the lovely valley of the River Yealm. One of its interesting buildings, Fardel, was formerly owned by Sir Walter Raleigh but there are other interesting granite houses to be seen. About 2½ miles south-west of Cornwood, near the village of Sparkwell, is the Dartmoor Wildlife Park where a variety of wild animals can be seen in semi-naturalistic surroundings. As usual, there are picnic areas, a gift shop, adventure playground, and a self-service restaurant.

Cranmere Pool
(191) (SX 6085) 6 miles S of Okehampton
Situated in the heart of northern Dartmoor close to the sources of the River Dart and the West Okement River, Cranmere Pool is one of the remoter spots on the moor. It is, however, the site of Dartmoor's oldest and perhaps best-known 'letterboxes' and attracts those who want to sign the visitor's book in the little cairn which was first built by James Perrot, the Dartmoor

The 'letterbox' at Cranmere Pool.

Dartington Hall, the centre for Dartington Arts.

guide, in 1854. The area is reputed to be haunted by the ghost of Bengie Geare, a mayor of Okehampton in the seventeenth century, who was convicted of sheep stealing and hanged nearby. His spirit was supposed to have been banished to the Pool where he was obliged to sip its waters until the Pool was drained. Suffice it to say, that there is no pool there now and only a sometimes treacherous bog remains!

Crediton
(191) (SS 8300) 6 miles W of Exeter
Crediton is named after the River Creedy and it is situated at the confluence of that river and the Yeo. Creedy is probably derived from a Celtic word meaning 'winding one' which appropriately describes the course of the river even today. Crediton was the birth place of St Boniface, the eighth-century English monk who became a missionary in Germany. Although Crediton has enjoyed a worthy history, its one remaining building of note is the imposing church by the main road. Crediton is on **Tour 2**.

Crockern Tor
(191) (SX 6175) 2 miles SW of Postbridge
Just to the north of the B3212 road, there is a low tor which was the meeting place of the stannary parliaments between 1474 and 1786. It is suggested that there were once granite seats there for the use of the parliament's members. On **Tour 4**.

Cullompton
(192) (SY 0107) 10 miles NE of Exeter
Situated by the River Culm and bypassed by the M5 motorway, Cullompton, like so many in South Devon, was once a wealthy wool town but most of the older buildings have been destroyed by a succession of serious fires, the earliest recorded being in 1602. The Church of St Andrew, dating mainly from the fifteenth century is one of the finest examples of a Perpendicular church in the county with a beautiful roof and rood screen.

Dart Valley Steam Railway see Buckfastleigh

Dartington Hall
(202) (SX 7962) 2 miles NW of Totnes
Dartington Hall dates back to the fourteenth century but, until it was bought by the Elmhirst family in 1925, it had fallen into rack and ruin. Its courtyard and Great Hall are medieval, and there are landscaped gardens. Now it is the centre for Dartington Arts, a registered charity whose aim is to promote the arts in the area. Meals are available in the White Hart Dining Room and there is a bar. Dartington Hall can be visited by taking a short diversion from **Tour 5**.

Dartmeet
(191) (SX 6773) 4 miles SE of Two Bridges
Dartmeet is a popular tourist attraction and beauty spot on the B3357 road at the point where the East and West Dart Rivers meet. The single-span clapper bridge here dates from some

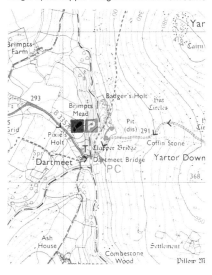

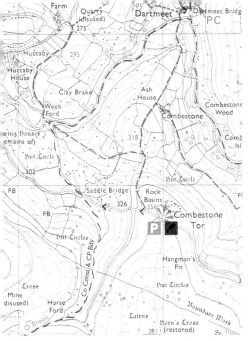

time between the thirteenth and fifteenth centuries. There is a large free car park, riverside walks and strolls, and Badger's Holt offers a gift shop, café, and small, exotic bird aviary. Dartmeet is on **Tour 4** and is the starting point for **Walk 10**.

Dartmoor Centre see Okehampton

Dartmoor National Park
The 365 square miles of Dartmoor National Park have been described as 'southern England's last wilderness'. The heather-clad granite up-

Dartmeet, the point where the East and West Dart rivers meet.

lands with their exposed knobs of rocks, the tors, carved by weathering and erosion into weird and wonderful shapes, are mostly privately owned but, in 1950, the National Park, together with nine others in England and Wales was established following the National Parks and Access to the Countryside Act in 1949. The National Park Authority, from its headquarters at Parke, near Bovey Tracey ★, is faced with the challenge of reconciling the sometimes conflicting interests of landowners, farmers, tourists, special interest groups, developers, conservationists, councils, the army, and others — not an easy task but one that they seem to manage splendidly. The National Park Rangers and Information Centres at strategic points are there to help visitors make the most of any trip to the area and, at the same time, preserve the moor and its animal, plant, and human life. The rangers maintain rights of way, try to keep Dartmoor tidy and safe, and help visitors to understand the way the moor works. They cannot, however, be everywhere at once so it is up to visitors always to behave in a responsible way.

With more and more people penetrating the moor's hinterland, there are risks both to the moor and to the visitors themselves. It has been reported. for example, that a Dartmoor pony bled to death following a cut it received to its mouth from inadvertently biting the ring-pull top of a drink can that had been tossed carelessly into the heather. On the other hand, even experienced walkers have been known to fall into the so-called 'feather beds' — water-filled clefts in the granite topped with an all-too-solid-looking blanket of sphagnum moss.

The Park Authority publishes a free annual newspaper *The Dartmoor Visitor* which is packed with advice and information. The Authority organizes guided walks and they also provide information about access and rights of way — inexperienced or improperly equipped visitors should never venture into the wilder parts of the moor. It is worth remembering, too, that the

The inner harbour, Dartmouth.

Ministry of Defence occupies a large training area on the northern part of the moor. The firing ranges are marked by red and white posts and by notice boards on the main approaches — again, an information leaflet is available from Information Centres. Dartmoor Information Centres can be found at Postbridge ★, Princetown ★, Tavistock ★, Steps Bridge ★, New Bridge ★, Okehampton ★, and Parke ★.

A good way to enjoy Dartmoor is on horseback and there are many excellent riding stables in the area where it is usually possible to find a horse to suit your age, weight, and level of experience. You should not need to worry about special clothing for riding although you must wear a hard hat (these are usually available from the stable but it is worth checking first). Do avoid wearing trousers or jeans with raised seams, and training shoes with smooth soles because these can easily slip out of the stirrups. You can usually book a short ride of about an hour or a trek of a whole day or more. The 'Leisure Activities' section on page 30 will provide more information on riding stables.

In general terms, there are several guidelines which the Authority asks visitors to adhere to. You should not feed the ponies or allow dogs to run loose among livestock. Nor should you camp by the roadside or drive off the road for more than 15 yards. Fire is always a risk, especially after a dry summer, so do not light camp fires or even barbecues unless you have special permission to do so, and do not throw down burning cigarettes or lighted matches. Wherever there are rights of way across the moor, there will be gates or stiles through boundary walls; there is no need to climb walls, therefore, so don't do it because they are easily damaged. And finally, don't dam any streams or rivers, or pollute the water in any way.

Dartmoor Wildlife Park see Cornwood

Dartmouth
(202) (SX 8751) 8 miles SE of Totnes
Because of its deep-water, well-protected harbour, Dartmouth has been an important port since Roman times and, in 1147, a fleet went out from Dartmouth to join the Second Crusade. Even in modern times, Dartmouth has earned its place in naval history for, in 1944, no fewer than 500 ships left the port for Normandy and the D-day Landings. It was from the thirteenth century, however, that the port began to flourish because of the wine trade with Bordeaux in France. The mouth of the River Dart is guarded by Dartmouth Castle built by Henry VII for coastal defence and added to towards the end of the sixteenth century. It is now owned by English Heritage and is open to the public throughout the year. The seventeenth-century Butterwalk in the town centre has a historical and maritime museum in a merchant's house built about 1640. There is a number of other interesting buildings including the eighteenth-century Mansion House in St George's Square and the Newcomen Engine House in Mayors Avenue which contains one of Thomas Newcomen's beam engines built in the early part of the eighteenth century for use in the Cornish tin mines and still in working order.

The wooded hill of Gallant's Bower at the back of Dartmouth Castle is owned by the National Trust and has a network of paths as well as an earthwork dating from the Civil War. About 3 miles west of Dartmouth, on the B3207 road near Blackawton is the Woodland Leisure Park. Here there are more than 50 acres of woodland and deer park, an 'Animal Farm', a café, and a shop where such items as honey, cakes, preserves or even large wooden dressers can be purchased. There is a story that in Monks Pool here in 1844, the body of a girl called Laura, who had been married only three weeks, was

47

Kingswear Station on the Dartmouth Steam Valley Railway.

found standing bolt upright — her ghost still haunts the pool they say! Dartmouth is on **Tour 6** and **Walk 3** begins on the other side of the Dart estuary at Kingswear.

Dartmouth Steam Valley Railway see Paignton

Dawlish

(192) (SX 9676) 1 mile NE of Teignmouth
Dawlish gets its name from the Dawlish Water which divides the town and the area known as the Lawn, and 'dawlish' comes from a Celtic word meaning 'black stream'. It is a popular family resort offering plenty to do for everyone as well as a long, sandy beach, and a number of sheltered coves perfect for sunbathing and swimming. The museum has interesting displays of toys and dolls, local history and trades, and not far away on the Exe estuary is Dawlish Warren Nature Reserve with large numbers of shore birds. **Tour 3** goes through Dawlish.

The railway station at Dawlish is practically on the beach.

Denbury

(202) (SX 8268) 3 miles SW of Newton Abbot
An unprepossessing village at first sight, lying beneath the site of Denbury Camp on the hill to the south-west. Its manor house is hidden by its great surrounding walls and is privately owned. But it is the church which offers the main interest. The first thing to strike the visitor is the statue in the churchyard of a boyscout with raised hand. This is a most unusual tombstone in memory of Thomas Peter Butler who died in 1932 at the young age of twenty-four.

The building of the church itself was completed in 1291. Notice the single-handed clock on the north face of the tower — it was made

This tombstone, in memory of Thomas Peter Butler, can be found in the churchyard at Denbury.

Denbury Church.

about 1730. Most exciting, however, is the fact that, at the time of Edward the Confessor, the manor of Denbury belonged to a Saxon monk, Aeldred, who eventually became Archbishop of York. In 1066, it was Aeldred who was called to place the Crown of England on the head of William the Conqueror in place of the Archbishop of Canterbury who had been exiled to France! Denbury is visited on **Tour 5.**

Dittisham

(202) (SX 8655) 3 miles N of Dartmouth
Situated on the steep valley side of the west bank of the River Dart, Dittisham (pronounced Ditsum) is a most attractive village with its stone and thatch houses in the narrow lanes. Dittisham is on **Tour 6.**

Drake's Island see Plymouth

Drewsteignton

(191) (SX 7391) 4 miles NE of Chagford
This is a charming Devon village built around a square at the head of which is the parish church. Anyone visiting the village — which is close to

Fingle Bridge (top) *and the Drew Arms* (above) *at Drewsteignton.*

both Castle Drogo ★ and to the picturesque setting of the sixteenth-century Fingle Bridge over the Teign — should call into the village pub, the Drew Arms. Here you can help yourself to drinks from the kitchen (there is no bar) and just leave your money on the table. Home-cooked snacks are also available. Drewsteignton is visited on **Tour 2.**

Dunsford

(191) (SX 8189) 8 miles W of Exeter
Situated just within the north-eastern boundary

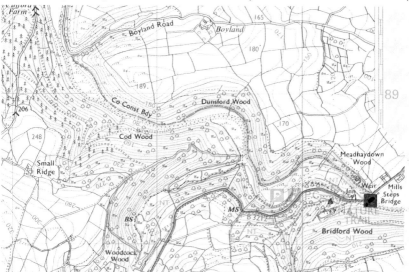

East Portlemouth.

East Portlemouth

(202) (SX 7438) 6 miles S of Kingsbridge
Situated on the opposite bank of the Salcombe
Estuary from Salcombe ★ itself, in medieval
times, East Portlemouth was a busy port, gradually giving way in importance to Salcombe as
ship-building was moved across the water. The
ships were built from local oak and used to
transport stone from quarries nearby. East
Portlemouth is a charming little village today,
and the drive along the estuary into Southpool
Creek and Waterhead Creek towards Chivelstone offers some lovely scenery. East
Portlemouth is on **Tour 7**.

of Dartmoor National Park, and close to the
River Teign, Dunsford is worth a look to inspect
the cottages of thatch and Devon cob as well as
the church of St Mary. The attractive Steps
Bridge is close by where there are several riverside strolls. Dunsford is on **Tour 2**.

Exeter Cathedral.

Exeter

(192) (SX 9292)
Celia Fiennes, the seventeenth-century travel
writer said of Exeter 'This Citty does exceed-
ingly resemble London...' and, while it may not
now be on the scale of England's capital, it is
worthy of being the county of Devon's principal
city. Like most major cities everywhere, Exeter
offers all the usual tourist facilities but, at the
same time, because it is comparatively com-

pact, there is not the same feeling of being 'hemmed in' that prevails in some of the more sprawling developments, and there is, too, a real sense of history.

The city dates from Roman times when it was the most important settlement for the Dumnonii tribe of Britons. It remains essentially a walled city with more than 75 per cent of its third-century, Roman wall still more-or-less intact, and it is possible to see many of Exeter's most interesting parts by following a walk around the walls — a distance of about 1½ miles. Although the distance is not great, you should allow at least 2 hours for the walk because there is a

Exeter City Walls.

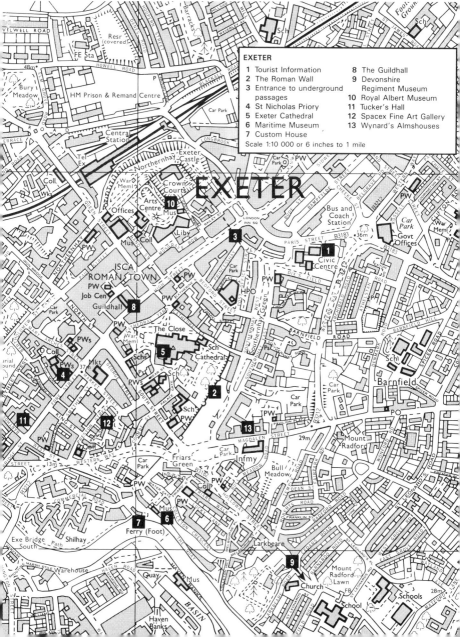

EXETER

1 Tourist Information
2 The Roman Wall
3 Entrance to underground passages
4 St Nicholas Priory
5 Exeter Cathedral
6 Maritime Museum
7 Custom House
8 The Guildhall
9 Devonshire Regiment Museum
10 Royal Albert Museum
11 Tucker's Hall
12 Spacex Fine Art Gallery
13 Wynard's Almshouses

Scale 1:10 000 or 6 inches to 1 mile

good deal to see.

The underground passages, entered from the Princesshay shopping precinct, are open to the public throughout the year from Tuesday to Saturday. They are part of a medieval water supply built to provide the cathedral, central Exeter, and St Nicholas Priory. The Cathedral Church of St Peter in Cathedral Close dominates the city and dates from the thirteenth century although, earlier, there was a Saxon minster on the same site. St Nicholas Priory in Mint Lane was part of a Benedictine monastery which dated from the eleventh century until the Dissolution.

No visit to Exeter would be complete without a visit to the Maritime Museum on The Quay, the old port. Here there is the world's largest collection of boats, some still afloat, as well as the usual tourist facilities, and it is very much a 'please touch' exhibition. Here, too, is the elegant, seventeenth-century Customs House. Other places of interest include the Guildhall,

which is the oldest municipal building in the country, the Devonshire Regiment Museum, the Royal Albert Museum, the Tuckers' Hall, The Spacex fine art gallery, and Wynards Almshouses as well as Quayside Crafts where you can find an exhibition and sale of more than fifty craft workers. It is worth remembering that, as well as being a port, Exeter has had a long association with the wool industry and Tuckers Hall, with its Jacobean panelling and fifteenth-century roof timbers, is still the Hall of the Incorporation of Weavers, Fullers and Shearmen.

The Northcott Theatre in the grounds of the University on Stocker Road about a mile from

The Customs House (below), *the Maritime Museum* (bottom), *and Parliament Street, the narrowest street in the world* (right), *Exeter.*

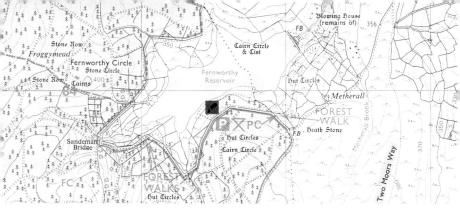

the city centre is a professional regional theatre offering a variety of live entertainment and films. Touring opera and dance companies also visit the theatre on a regular basis. During May and June Exeter Festival is devoted to music, the theatre, art, and Devon folk history. Exeter is the starting point for **Tours 2** and **3**.

Exmouth
(192) (SY 0080) 8 miles SE of Exeter
Regular visitors to Devon will not be surprised to learn that Exmouth has been a holiday resort longer than any other in Devon. Situated on the eastern bank of the River Exe estuary, it offers over 2 miles of sands so that it is a favourite with children. On the sea front, there is The Wonderful World of Miniature which proudly boasts the world's largest 00 Model Railway Complex, and, in buildings that were once stables, there is Exmouth Museum which concentrates on local history. In Foxholes Road, there is a nineteenth-century building — now the Barn Hotel — which has been described as one of the most important buildings of its date in Europe — its plan is in the shape of a butterfly!

Just around the coast from Exmouth itself is Sandy Bay where there is the Country Life Museum. Privately owned, it offers a deer park, a stables and pets paddock, exhibitions of vintage cars and farm machinery, as well as the usual tourist facilities. Exmouth is visited on **Tour 1**.

Fernworthy Reservoir
(191) (SX 6684) 4 miles SW of Chagford
Fernworthy Reservoir is a large (76 acres) body of water in a lovely setting and held in the grasp of Fernworthy Forest, first planted in the 1920s and now managed jointly by the Forestry Commission, Dartmoor National Park Authority, and the South-west Water Authority. It is a place to come to walk through the network of paths created by the Commission or to fish in peace and quiet. On the south-western side of the reservoir, a Special Protection Zone for birds has been set up where the Devon Birdwatching and Preservation Society has a hide. The water is stocked with brown trout so that there is excellent fly fishing to be had here either from the bank or from Bristol boats. At certain times of the year, however, the area can seem remarkably bleak. A short diversion from **Tour 8**.

Finch Foundry Museum see Okehampton

Forde House see Newton Abbot

Fursdon House
(192) (SX 9204) 9 miles N of Exeter
Fursdon House, situated in some 700 acres of parkland and informal gardens between the village of Cadbury and the banks of the River Exe remains the family home of the Fursdon family who have owned the estate since the twelfth century. The present manor house has a fine Georgian front, a Regency library, panelled dining room, and even a family museum. Visits can be arranged at any time of the year by prior booking.

Gidleigh
(191) (SX 6788) 2 miles W of Chagford
Gidleigh is a tiny village tucked away among the rolling, heather-clad folds of northern Dartmoor. It boasts a tiny Norman castle and a lovely church. **Tour 8** passes close to Gidleigh.

Gorse Blossom Miniature Railway Park see Newton Abbot

Grimspound
(191) (SX 7080) 5 miles NW of Postbridge
With its perimeter wall clearly visible as well as the remains of several round huts, Grimspound

Grimspound.

is perhaps the best-known archaeological site on Dartmoor. It is thought to be the remains of a Bronze Age village. On **Walk 8**.

Harberton

(202) (SX 7758) 2 miles SW of Totnes
There are so many delightful villages in this part of South Devon, so why single out this one? Perhaps it is because the old and the new sit cheek by jowl, because there is a fine Perpendicular church looking down over the village, and because, close by, the Church House Inn offers hospitality, fine food, and a fascinating interior. In the centre of the village there is a working farm, and morning and evening the cattle can be seen being driven up and down the village street for milking.

Harberton.

Hayes Barton

(192) (SY 0585) 3 miles NW of Budleigh Salterton
It was here, in this splendid Tudor farmhouse, that Walter Raleigh was born in 1552. Although, it is only occasionally open to the public, it can be viewed easily from the road.

Haytor

(191) (SX 7577) 4 miles W of Bovey Tracey
Situated close to the B3387, Bovey Tracey ★ road, Haytor rocks must be one of the most popular granite tors on Dartmoor. At least part of its fame stems from the nearby remains of the

The Granite Tramway (top), *and the rocks* (above), *at Haytor.*

Haytor Granite Tramway, a stone-built railway engineered in 1820 by George Templer to carry stone from the Dartmoor quarries to the Stover Canal at Ventiford and thence via the canal and river to Teignmouth ★ . Even the points are made of stone. Granite from this area was used to build what was once one of London's most famous landmarks, London Bridge. George Templer succeeded in frittering away his own and a good deal of the family's fortune (built up by the first James Templer in the eighteenth century) and was finally killed in a hunting accident in 1843, leaving the family's position much lowlier than that which he had inherited. The village of Haytor Vale is situated below the rocks. On **Tour 4**.

Haytor Vale see Haytor

Higher Uppacott Dartmoor Longhouse

(191) (SX 7072) 4 miles SW of Widecombe
The Dartmoor Longhouse of Higher Uppacott near Poundsgate is one of the few largely unaltered examples of a Longhouse remaining on Dartmoor. The medieval dwelling has a thatched roof and was built so that humans and their domestic stock could be housed in the same building. The living quarters were at a higher level than the cowshed giving rise to the Longhouse's characteristic sloping shape. Higher

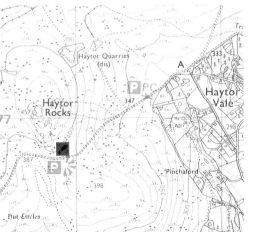

Holne.

Uppacott probably dates from the fourteenth century. It may be visited either from one of the guided walks arranged by the National Park Authority or by booking a visit directly with the Authority (see 'Leisure Activities').

Holne

(202) (SX 7069) 4 miles NW of Buckfastleigh

Holne is another one of the delightful Dartmoor-edge villages. Charles Kingsley had the good fortune to be born at the vicarage in 1819 while his father was curate in charge of St Mary the Virgin village church. The church was probably built in the thirteenth century and was then enlarged in the 1400s. Nearby is one more of the splendid Church House Inns so common in this area. Holne is on **Tour 4**.

Honiton

(192) (ST 1600)

The town was founded by the fifth Earl of Devon, William de Vernon, in the twelfth century although, because of the fires which have ravaged this like so many other Devon towns, there is little left which is older than the mid-1700s. It

has been famous for lace-making since the sixteenth century, and in Allhallows Museum there is a fine display of Honiton lace as well as various items of local history. There is also a working pottery in the town where visitors can watch tableware and cookware being made. Honiton is on **Tour 1**.

Hope Cove

(202) (SX 6740) 5 miles W of Salcombe

The first written record of Hope Cove dates back to an Assizes Roll of 1281 in which it was called La Hope. It has been famous and infamous for its fishing and its smuggling but now it is a popular little resort with a safe bathing beach. Its thatched cottages and Old Lifeboat Station add to its appeal. **On Tour 7**.

Hound Tor

(191) (SX 7479) 5 miles W of Bovey Tracey

As well as being a fine example of a granite tor, close by Hound Tor there is one of the best-

Hound Tor (below) *and Hope Cove* (bottom).

known examples of a ruined medieval village to be seen on Dartmoor. And archaeologists have even discovered evidence of an earlier wattle and turf village beneath the stone houses. Hound Tor is on **Walk 7**.

Ivybridge
(202) (SX 6356)
Situated just outside the southern boundary of the Dartmoor National Park, the town gets its name from the thirteenth-century packhorse bridge over the River Erme. It grew up mainly in the nineteenth century because a paper-making industry was sited there to make use of the waters of the Erme. On **Tour 9**.

The Shambles, Kingsbridge.

Kents Cavern see Torquay

Killerton House
(192) (SS 9700) 8 miles N of Exeter
Killerton Park is situated on the east bank of the River Culme, and was given to the National Trust by Sir Richard Acland in 1944 — the estate had been the ancestral home of his family since the English Civil War. It is now the National Trust's regional headquarters. Although this Georgian house has no special architectural merit, the hillside gardens and park are splendid, offering lovely walks at most times of the year. One of the most imporant features of the house is the exhibition of costumes from the eighteenth century up to the present, and displayed in room settings.

Kingsbridge
(202) (SX 7344) 12 miles SW of Totnes
Kingsbridge is a busy but attractive market town situated at the head of the Kingsbridge estuary in the southern part of the South Hams District, and gets its name because of the bridge which joined two Royal estates. Its Royal Charter dates back to 962 and it was given a market at the beginning of the thirteenth century. Kingsbridge still has its own town crier. The Cookworthy Museum in Fore Street takes its name from William Cookworthy who discovered hard paste porcelain in the eighteenth century. The building is a seventeenth-century school house — the Old Grammar School. It has a variety of local history displays including a Victorian pharmacy and kitchen. Also in Fore Street is the Shambles Arcade which is well worth a look (a shambles, incidentally, was a slaughterhouse or a butcher's stall). The Kingsbridge Miniature Railway is a 7½ inch gauge railway which runs for ½ mile along the Quay and is capable of carrying passengers. The locomotive, *Heidi*, is powered by a battery-driven electric motor.

About 6 miles to the north of Kingsbridge,

Safe moorings in Kingsbridge harbour.

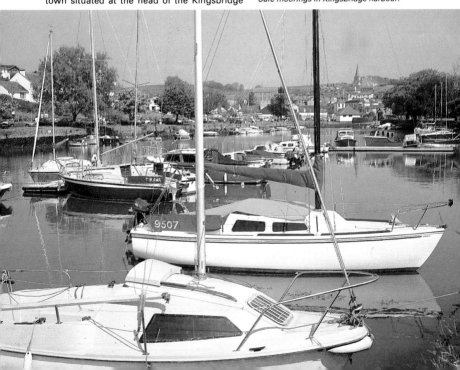

The beautiful Lydford Gorge.

between Loddiswell village and California Cross just off the old B3196 road, is Loddiswell Vineyard. (The place name of Loddiswell, incidentally, is thought to derive from 'Our Lady's Well'.) This is a working English vineyard producing high-quality wine based mainly on German white grapes (in fact, in the fine summer of 1989, the owner claimed to have been visited by German shippers with a view to exporting Loddiswell wine to Germany). Guided tours of the vineyard and winery are available or visitors may walk unaccompanied around just the vineyard. Needless to say, tastings can be arranged, too, and wine can be purchased from the shop. Kingsbridge is on **Tour 7**.

Kirkham House see Paignton

Kitley Caves
(202) (SX 5751) 6 miles E of Plymouth
These extensive limestone caverns, situated in the attractive valley of the River Yealm (pronounced 'Yam') are the only caves in Devon outside of the Torbay area. The cave research team based here continue to explore the system, and visitors may wander freely throughout those parts of the caverns which have been illuminated. The rock formations are both beautiful and dramatic and, for the scientifically minded, there is a centre for cave science which has its own museum. There is also a gift shop, woodland trail, and children's play area. The caves are open from the Spring Bank Holiday through to the end of September. A short diversion from **Tour 9**.

Lichway
The Lichway was an ancient track which led right across Dartmoor to the church in Lydford. The prefix 'lich' is thought to derive from an Old English word *lic*, meaning a 'body or corpse' so that the Lichway is also known as the Way of the Dead. In other words, it was a route which was used to bring the dead from various parts of the moor to Lydford for burial at a time when a large part of Dartmoor was contained within the parish. In fact, despite its name, the track must also have been used by people coming for baptisms, weddings, and other church ceremonies. It is still possible to trace parts of the route.

Loddiswell Vineyard see Kingsbridge

Lustleigh
(191) (SX 7881) 3 miles NW of Bovey Tracey
The village of Lustleigh lies in the beautiful wood valley of the the River Bovey. Grouped around the church, there are most attractive fifteenth- and sixteenth-century stone and thatch buildings, although the village seems to have extended now along the road as more people have discovered the delights of living in such a lovely Devon valley. It is possible that Lustleigh was a place of Christian worship before the thirteenth century. In the eighteenth century, a curate of the parish church spent almost fifty years writing and printing the twenty-six volumes of a work entitled *A System of Divinity*. Lustleigh is on **Tour 4**.

Lydford
(191) (SX 5184) 8 miles N of Tavistock
A short diversion from **Tour 8** will take you to the little village of Lydford where, close by the church, the first building to attract one's attention is Lydford Castle. This was first built in 1195 as a prison and is a modest, freestanding tower of two stories. It was rebuilt in the thirteenth

century when a ditch was dug around the tower and soil piled up around the ground-floor walls. The upper stories were rebuilt and the interior of the ground floor filled in.

The Saxon church of St Petroc was rebuilt in the thirteenth century, too, although an earlier church, sacked by the Danes in 997, had stood on the site since 650. About a half a mile down the road is the spectacular Lydford Gorge owned by the National Trust. It is the best example in the south-west of river capture and the most remarkable gorge west of of Cheddar. In places, the moss-hung walls of the gorge are 60 feet high and, after heavy rain, water boils through the narrow ravine. The 100-foot White Lady Waterfall and the Devil's Cauldron are described in the National Trust's promotional material as '...an unforgettable adventure for all the family...'; this is no overstatement!

Lydford Gorge see Lydford

Lympstone
(192) (SX 9984) 1 mile N of Exmouth
Sandwiched between the busy A376 road and the banks of the River Exe, Lympstone appears to be an odd mix of the old and the new with white-painted, thatched cottages beside Victorian Torrington or red brick, beside stucco. The railway between Exeter and Exmouth seems to add to the oddness of the village by being carried above the houses on tall viaducts. The narrow passages leading down to the river between leaning buildings seem a little intimidating at first but, if you do venture into them, you will find quaint buildings which seem almost to be tumbling down into the water. It is worth walking along the privately owned wall to the tiny harbour from where a better view may be obtained of the village bending over the Exe.

Note the clock tower erected in 1885 by W H Peters of Harefield in memory of his beloved wife Mary Jane to commemorate her kindness and sympathy for the poor of the village. By modern tastes, the red-brick Victorian tower is hardly a beautiful monument but one cannot help but speculate on the devotion, love, wealth, and power that lay behind the memorial. It is known as the Peter Tower. On **Tour 1**.

The clock tower, known as the Peter Tower, Lympstone.

Wooded Dartmoor, near Manaton.

Manaton
(191) (SX 7580) 5 miles NW of Bovey Tracey
On the hill above the village, the church of St Winifred's looks down upon Manaton. Situated in a more thickly wooded area of Dartmoor, Manaton also has an attractive village green.

Mary Tavy
(191) (SX 5079) 4 miles N of Tavistock
This village by the Tavy, with its church dedicated to St Mary, is roughly twice the size of its east-bank twin, Peter Tavy ★. It is in the heart of Dartmoor's lead-, tin-, and copper-mining country, and the famous National Trust engine house remains of Wheal Betsy ★ is only a mile to the north alongside the A386. On **Tour 8**.

Wheal Betsy, Mary Tavy.

Mearsdon Manor see Moretonhampstead

Miniature Pony Centre see Moretonhampstead

Modbury
(202) (SX 6551) 3 miles SW of Ivybridge
Situated astride the A379 road on a steep hill, Modbury is an attractive little market and residential town with some Georgian elegance and a medieval church with a spire. The barracks, where the troops trained to fight Napoleon were housed, still stand, and there is also the neo-classical Literary and Scientific Institute founded in 1840 by Richard King. Modbury has its annual fair and carnival in May. On **Tour 9**.

Moretonhampstead
(191) (SX 7586) 12 miles SE of Okehampton
Moretonhampstead is a typical Dartmoor town, now favoured as a centre for exploring the moor but once an important market. The church dates back to the fifteenth century and the seventeenth-century almshouses have fine solid granite pillars. The thirteenth-century Mearsdon Manor in Cross Street now houses a gallery exhibiting jade, ebony, copper, and water colours from all over the world. Three miles southwest of Moretonhampstead on the B3212 Princetown Road is The Miniature Pony Centre which holds one of the largest studs of miniature ponies in the world with over 100 individual animals. With pedigrees dating from 1890, some of these pure-bred ponies are very rare. As well as the pony paddocks, there is a goat paddock, a piggery, kennels, a display of ornamental birds, a picnic area, and restaurant. On **Tour 2**.

Morwellham Quay see Tavistock

National Shire Horse Centre
(202) (SX5951) 8 miles E of Plymouth
The National Shire Horse Centre near Yealmpton (pronounced Yampton) claims to be one of the most popular tourist attractions in Devon. It is open to the public throughout the year and visitors may have a close look at more than thirty-five of these great horses and their foals, as well as taking cart rides, watching a traditional smith at work, or seeing the spectacular flying displays of eagles and other birds of prey. There is also a butterfly house, adventure playground, craft centre, restaurant, and more besides. There are special events held here from time to time, such as steam rallies or medieval fayres. On **Tour 9**.

New Bridge
(202) (SX 711708) 4 miles W of Ashburton
Despite its name, the granite pack horse bridge which spans the lovely River Dart here, was built in the fifteenth century as part of a series of Bridges linking south-east Dartmoor to Tavistock. The triangular refuges in the single-track bridge were originally designed to allow foot travellers to keep out of the way of the fast-

St Leonard's Tower, Newton Abbot.

moving pack horses — today, it is cars from which pedestrians seek protection. A little under a mile to the north-west of New Bridge is Aish Tor, and running in a south-westerly direction under the tor is Dr Blackall's Drive, a track built by a Doctor T Blackall of Exeter so that his wife could be driven in pony and trap across the moor when she became unable to walk it. It now forms part of one of a series of walks in the area for which a leaflet is available from the National Park authority.

Newton Abbot
(202) (SX 8671)
Each Wednesday throughout the year, livestock and local produce are brought to Newton Abbot for sale in the local market. This has been happening, largely uninterrupted for about 700 years! In fact, the first Wednesday market was held by the Abbots in 1220 with the permission of Henry III. Newton Abbot has been described as the 'gateway to Dartmoor and the coast' but

The railway station, Newton Abbot.

it still has a busy life of its own as well as offering many tourist facilities, including horse racing and stock car racing at the racecourse and sailing and fishing in Decoy Lake. In the centre of the town is a clock tower; this is St Leonard's Tower and is all that has survived of the chapel dedicated to that saint which once stood on the site. It was from the steps of the tower that the first declaration of William of Orange was read in 1688.

Just to the west of the town, between the A381 and A383 roads is Bradley Manor set among lovely woods. Its history dates back to 1250 although the present building is largely fifteenth century. It is in the hands of the National Trust and is open to the public between April and September.

Forde House was built during the reign of James I in the style of a sixteenth-century mansion. About 4 miles north of Newton Abbot is Gorse Blossom Miniature Railway and Woodland Park set among 35 acres of oak woodland — it is ideal for children and parents alike. Newton Abbot is visited on **Tour 5**.

Newton Ferrers
(201) (SX 5448) 6 miles SE of Plymouth
Newton Ferrers, with its twin village of Noss Mayo, sit on either side of the lovely Yealm

(pronounced 'Yam') estuary. They are both picture postcard villages and are beloved by artists. On **Tour 9**.

North Brentor
(191) (SX 4881) 5 miles N of Tavistock
The main reason to visit North Brentor is to go to the village church of St Michael de Rupe on Brent Tor itself about a mile to the south-west. Built in 1130, it stands on the top of the remains of a volcanic cone. There is a legend that it was originally planned to build the church at the foot of the hill but that, as the stones were placed, the devil took them to the top of the hill every night so that, in the end, the builders had to complete their work where Lucifer dictated. There are picnic site, car park, and toilets here. Brent Tor could be visited by taking a short diversion from **Tour 8**.

Noss Mayo see Newton Ferrers

Okehampton
(191) (SX 5895)
Okehampton lies just outside the northern boundary of Dartmoor and is a good centre for exploring this part of the moor. Until the Okehampton bypass was completed, after years of controversy about whether it should be routed north or south of the town, the old A30 passed through the Town's High Street and was a notorious bottleneck for traffic heading on to Cornwall. Even today, High Street is still busy with local and tourist vehicles but is still dominated by St James's Church which, despite its small size, has an impressive fourteenth-century tower.

Okehampton owes its origins to the castle built by a Norman Sheriff of Devon in 1086 to put down a rebellion in south-west England, but

Left and below: *the lovely Yealm Estuary at Newton Ferrers and Noss Mayo.*

Okehampton Castle

the castle was dismantled in the mid-sixteenth century. Okehampton Castle is about a mile to the south-west of the present town, and the ruins are well worth a visit — they are said to be haunted!

Okehampton is an excellent shopping centre offering local produce as well as the usual goods to be had anywhere. There is plenty of accommodation and the Dartmoor Centre in West Street houses the Museum of Dartmoor Life which is run by a charitable trust. The museum occupies an early nineteenth-century mill and warehouse, while the Dartmoor and West Devon Information Centre is in the old printer's works in the courtyard of the museum. The West Okement River runs through the town and, just to the south, there is a golf course which welcomes visiting golfers. Here, too, there is a pleasant park, although Simmons Park, in the town, has the usual recreational facilities.

At Sticklepath ★ , about 4 miles to the east of Okehampton centre is the Finch Foundry Museum of Rural Industry which has a working water-powered edge tool works. Okehampton is the starting point for **Tour 8**.

Oldway Mansion see Paignton

Otterton Mill see Budleigh Salterton

Ottery St Mary
(192) (SY 0995) 10 miles W of Exeter
On the banks of the attractive River Otter and with a splendid thirteenth- and fourteenth-century church dedicated to St Mary and modelled on Exeter Cathedral, Ottery was the birthplace in 1772 of the poet Coleridge, whose father was

vicar here. A little to the north-west of the town is Cadhay Manor with an Elizabethan Long Gallery and part of a fifteenth-century timber roof. On **Tour 1**.

Cadhay Manor (above right) and the church of St Mary (right), Ottery St Mary

Kirkham House, Paignton.

Overbecks Museum and Garden see Salcombe

Paignton

(202) (SX 8960) 3 miles S of Torquay

Facing Tor Bay and at the heart of the English Riviera triangle, including Torquay ★ and Brixham ★, Paignton is a favourite family holiday resort not least because of its long, safe, sandy beaches. The old town is a little distance from the sea and, in Mill Lane off Cecil Road, there is Kirkham House, a stone-built Devon dwelling which may have been a priest's house. Oldway Mansion was built in 1873 by Isaac Singer of sewing machine fame and has a marble hall and stairway. The more usual tourist attractions include the Seashore Aquarium on South Quay, the Zoo on the Totnes Road, and the pier. The Torbay and Dartmouth Railway offers a steam train journey to Kingswear following the Torbay coast. On **Tour 6**.

Parke see Bovey Tracey

Pecorama Pleasure Park see Beer

Peter Tavy

(191) (SX 5177) 3 miles NE of Tavistock

Peter Tavy lies on the east bank of the River Tavy and, like its sister village Mary Tavy ★, was probably originally named simply, Tavy, after the river. The prefix stems from the saint to whom its parish church, dating back to about 1500, is dedicated. A good deal of restoration work was carried out to the church during the nineteenth century. The splendid village inn probably goes back to the early 1600s.

Pizwell see Postbridge

Plymouth

(201) (SX 4755)

Although Exeter ★ is its capital, Plymouth is Devon's largest city, much of it, on the outskirts, a sprawling suburbia little different from any

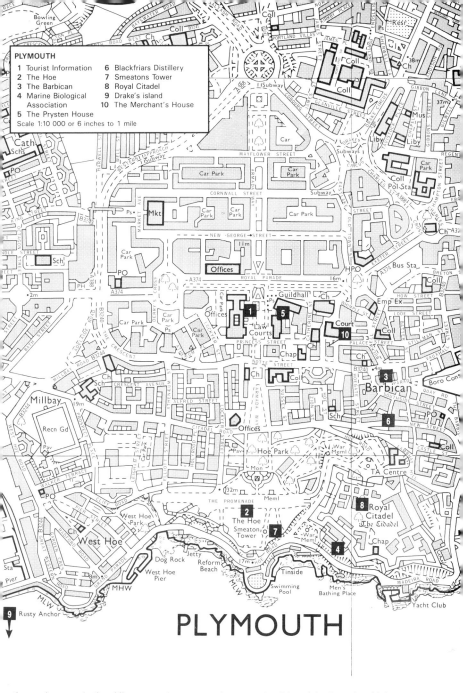

PLYMOUTH

1 Tourist Information	6 Blackfriars Distillery
2 The Hoe	7 Smeatons Tower
3 The Barbican	8 Royal Citadel
4 Marine Biological Association	9 Drake's island
5 The Prysten House	10 The Merchant's House

Scale 1:10 000 or 6 inches to 1 mile

PLYMOUTH

The Barbican (above left), *and the Hoe* (left), *Plymouth*

other major conurbation. Like many other ports in Britain, Plymouth suffered widespread destruction during World War II, and the city fathers rebuilt around that which survived in a way which, at first sight, seems to clash with the old but which in the end gives the city a style all its own. It must be Sir Francis Drake's game of bowls on the Hoe before setting off to wreak havoc on the ships of the Armada which everyone thinks of when Plymouth is mentioned. And, of course it was from Plymouth that the Pilgrim Fathers departed for America in the seventeenth century to found a New World Plymouth in 1620. There is still a bowling green on the Hoe and all of the historical events surrounding the city seem to be commemorated in its street names — anyone wishing to relive the events surrounding the ill-fated invasion of England might visit the 'Armada Experience' in

Prysten House (left), and the Guildhall (below left), Plymouth.

New Street among the narrow streets of the old Barbican.

There is a great deal to see in the city, from modern attractions, such as the Aquarium of the Marine Biological Association on the eastern end of the Hoe, to the Prysten House in Finewell Street, Royal Parade which is a late fifteenth-century priest's house, and possibly Plymouth's oldest building where the New World Tapestry, designed by Tom Mor depicts the founding of the Americas. You can take a tour of the Black Friars Distillery in Southside Street where Plymouth Gin is made or, again on the Hoe by the seafront, there is Smeaton's Tower, one of the lights which once stood, for 100 years, on the Eddystone Rocks. The Eddystone Rocks are 14 miles out to sea from the position of Smeaton's Tower today. The Royal Citadel is a seventeenth-century fort which now houses the 29th Commando Regiment of the Royal Artillery. Between May and September you can go to Drake's or St Nicholas's Island in Plymouth Sound which was a fortress and now offers an adventure centre with guns, tunnels, and underground ammunition stores. It was first recorded in the year 1135 and the fort was built and manned by gunners in 1549. Its name was changed from St Nicholas's Island to Drake's Island in 1590 in honour of the famous sea captain and it continued to be in the hands of the military until 1956. The present adventure centre is managed by the Mayflower Trust.

The Merchant's House Museum in St Andrew Street is a restored Tudor house dating from the sixteenth century and now has a museum of Plymouth social history. **Tours 9** and **10** start from Plymouth.

Postbridge
(191) (SX 6478) 5 miles NW of Princetown
The present little village of Postbridge, with a

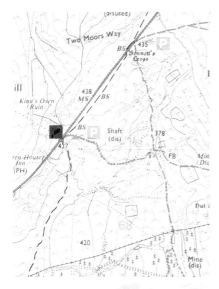

The thirteenth-century tenement, Pizwell (left), and the River Dart at Postbridge (above).

population of about 120, dates largely from the late eighteenth century when the toll road was built across the moor from Moretonhampstead ★ to Tavistock ★ . As well as the present road bridge, there is a ford here, and the fine clapper bridge across the East Dart River can be seen with its granite slabs laid across the stone piers — it is thought to date from the fourteenth century. There is an excellent National Park Information Centre in the public car park.

A couple of miles to the north-west is the Warren House Inn, claimed to be the third high-est pub in England. Two miles to the east of Postbridge, reached either by footpath or by turning on to the Widecombe road from the B3212, is the thirteenth-century tenement of Pizwell which is still a working farm. About 3 miles down the B3212 are the remains of the buildings which, in the nineteenth century, housed a gunpowder-manufacturing works — the so-called Powder Mills. By the side of the track can be seen the original mortar which was used to test the powder, and there is now a working pottery in one of the buildings. On **Tours 4** and **8**.

Powderham Castle

(192) (SX 9683) 4 miles N of Dawlish

Built between 1390 and 1420 by Sir Philip Courtenay, the Castle is still privately owned and lived in by the Earl of Devon, a direct descendant of Sir Philip. The Castle was damaged during the Civil War and underwent some alteration in the eighteenth and nineteenth centuries. It is

The Clapper Bridge (left), the Sheepfold (below), and Powder Mills (right), Postbridge.

Look out for the 160 year old tortoise in the grounds of Powderham Castle!

open to the public from May to September. There is a tortoise to be found ambling about the grounds which, it is claimed, is at least 160 years old! Nearby, the red breccia Powderham Church is a listed building of great historical interest. On **Tour 3**.

Powder Mills see Postbridge

Prawle Point
(202) (SX 7734) 8 miles S of Kingsbridge
The headland of Prawle Point is the most south-

PRAWLE POINT 78

erly extremity of South Devon. Its name is derived from a Saxon word meaning 'to peep' perhaps suggesting the long use of the point as a coastal lookout. Just below the point, in the fields on the wave-cut platform there are the remains of bunkers, part of the World War II coastal defence system. There is a National Trust car park near the point, and the whole of this stretch of magnificent coast is an ideal place for watching the soaring seabirds. The village of East Prawle, just to the north, offers hospitality in the form of two pubs, and is on **Tour 7**.

Princetown
(191) (SX 5873) 8 miles E of Tavistock
Most visitors to Princetown are there to see the forbidding-looking prison. It was Thomas Tyrwhitt, friendly with the Prince of Wales after whom the village is named, who in 1806 put forward the idea of building a prison there to house French prisoners of war. Hostilities between England and France had started up again in 1803 and, at first, prisoners of war were incarcerated in prison hulks at Plymouth which soon became overcrowded. Although it was a

The exciting coastline of Prawle Point.

The prison, Princetown.

prison and it is the highest above sea level in England. It was not until 1850 that the prison was used to incarcerate convicts from British justice after deportation of criminals was abolished in the 1840s. Dartmoor Prison now holds about 250 prisoners.

During the August Bank Holiday Week, visitors to Princetown can buy items made by the prisoners in their workshops at a sale held in the town hall. On **Tour 8**.

Prysten House see Plymouth

River Dart Country Park see Ashburton

Salcombe
(202) (SX 7439) 4 miles S of Kingsbridge
The superb Kingsbridge estuary, where Salcombe is sited at the most southerly tip, is fed by the Southpool, Frogmore, Collapit, Blanksmill, and Batson Creeks. The harbour, which is one of the safest on the south coast of England, has made Salcombe a famous fishing and yachting centre, and the Salcombe Town Regatta, first opened in 1857, offers sailing races as well as a fishing competition and a treasure hunt. The town, sloping steeply down to the sea,

government contractor who organized the building of the jail, the actual labour was carried out by the prisoners themselves. Perhaps it is hardly surprising, therefore, that it took three years before the prison was built. In 1813, the prison population was swollen still further by prisoners of war from the conflict between England and America between 1812 and 1814. Princetown jail's history as a place of confinement for prisoners of war continued until 1816 with the 100 Day's War following Napoleon's escape from Elba. Between then and the middle of the century, the jail stood empty.

The town of Princetown grew up around the

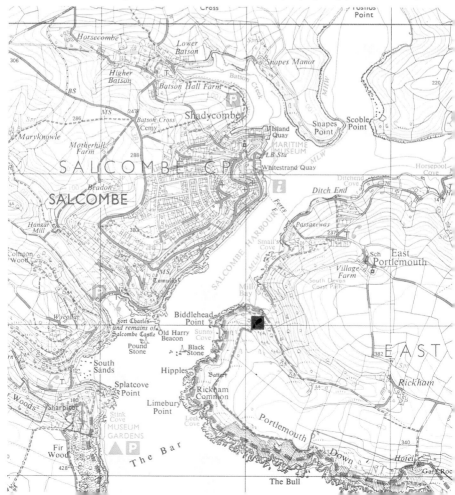

Near Mill Bay Cove, opposite Salcombe.

has quiet byways to explore as well as good shopping and tourist facilities. The Salcombe Maritime and Local History Museum in Cook's Boatstore, Custom's House, Quay on the waterfront is worth a visit but can only be approached on foot. At Sharpitor, 1½ miles south-west of the town centre is the Overbecks Museum and Garden run by the National Trust. The 6-acre garden offers fine views over Salcombe Harbour as well as some rare plants. There is a museum of ships and shipbuilding which also has a special children's exhibition of toys and dolls. On **Tour 7**.

Saltram House
(201) (SX 5255) 3½ miles E of Plymouth
Situated on the east bank of the River Plym between the A38 and A379 roads, Saltram House is a superb mansion from the period of George II in the mid-eighteenth century. Set in beautiful landscaped parkland, with its orangery and woodlands running down to the river, the house can boast two rooms designed by Robert Adams, portraits by Sir Joshua Reynolds, and some fine plasterwork and other decoration. The house is open to visitors on selected days between April and October. Even if you do not wish to visit the house, there is a circular walk possible in Saltram Park for which a leaflet is available from the National Trust.

Sand see Sidmouth

Seaton
(192) (SY 2490) 10 miles SE of Honiton
Whereas neighbouring Beer ★ remains an unspoiled fishing village, in the last 100 years Seaton, with its long pebble beach, has grown up into a busy holiday resort with all the attendant hotels, guest houses, caravan sites, and amusements. Despite that, there are still some interesting Victorian and Edwardian houses to be seen. The River Axe by which Seaton is situated is an important site for shore and wading birds. The Seaton Electric Tramway which runs from the Riverside Depot on Harbour Road will take you on a riverside ride along the Axe to Colyton ★ aboard narrow-gauge, open-top electric tramcars which are the last of their kind in the country. Seaton is on **Tour 1**.

Shaldon
(192) (SX 9272) ½ mile S of Teignmouth
The Georgian village of Shaldon is situated on the opposite bank of the River Teign from Teignmouth and a daily ferry connects the two places. On Wednesdays, local inhabitants dress in period costume. The Shaldon Wildlife Trust, on the headland known as the Ness, houses a collection of endangered small mammals, exotic birds, and reptiles.

Shute Barton see Axminster

The Gate House at Shute.

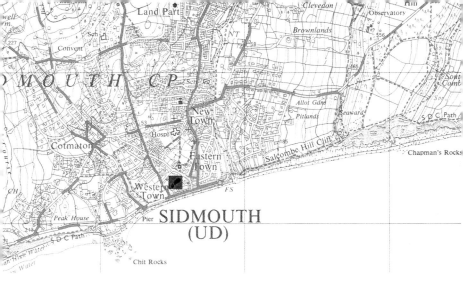

SIDMOUTH
(UD)

Sidmouth

(192) (SY 1287) 15 miles W of Exeter

Sidmouth remains an elegant Georgian and Regency coastal resort admirably represented by Fortfield Terrace, The Esplanade, and Coburg Terrace. It has a pebble beach but, nearby, there is the area called Jacob's ladder where there are sands and rock pools. Sidmouth Museum in Church Street has displays of Honiton lace, Victorian costumes, Regency prints, and so on. For children of all ages, there is the Vintage Toy and Train Museum in Field's Department Store in the Market Place exhibiting toys, such as electric trains and meccano, from a fifty-year period.

A couple of miles to the north of the town, in Sidbury, is Sand a fifteenth and sixteenth-century house still owned by the Huyshe family and open to the public on certain days from April to August. And the donkey sanctuary on the Sidford to Lyme Regis road, is also worth a visit. **On Tour 1**.

Silverlands see Chudleigh

Slapton Ley see Torcross

South Devon Heritage Coast

This is one of forty-three lengths of coastline around England and Wales which has been designated as Areas of Outstanding Natural Beauty by the Countryside Commission as well as of natural and historic interest. This stretch of Heritage Coast runs for 58 miles from Sharkham Point near Brixham ★ to Wembury Beach to the east of Plymouth ★ .Since 1984 it has been managed jointly by the South Hams District Council, Devon County Council, and the National Trust. The aims of the Management Service are to conserve the coast and, at the same time, to enable visitors to enjoy it without interfering with the interests of the local people. It is possible to obtain an attractive and informative package of Coast Path Guides for walkers and motorists from the Heritage Coast Office in Totnes.

The Esplanade (top), and the Old Chancel, Sidmouth.

South Hams

This is the name given to a district of South Devon which stretches from the River Dart in the east to the Tamar in the west and from Holne Moor in the southern part of Dartmoor to Prawle Point ★ on the southernmost tip of the coast. The name of the area is derived from on Old English word meaning 'a sheltered place' and was used to describe the settlements of this area as early as the middle of the ninth century. The main towns of the region are Totnes ★ ,

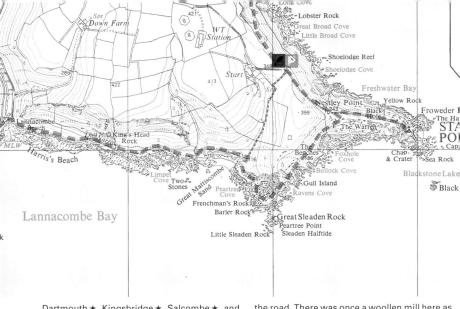

Dartmouth ★ , Kingsbridge ★ , Salcombe ★ , and Ivybridge ★ .

Start Point see **Tour 7** and **Walk 4**

Steps Bridge see Dunsford

Sticklepath
(191) (SX 6394) 4 miles E of Okehampton
The name 'Sticklepath' means simply 'steep path' and refers to a track which can still be traced up the hill west of the town parallel with the road. There was once a woollen mill here as well as a flour mill; these, together with the edging tools of what is now the Finch Foundry Museum ★ were driven by a total of seven waterwheels on the River Taw. Sticklepath has a number of claims to fame, at least one of which has its amusing side; in the eighteenth century, George III's carriage became stuck on the road bridge crossing the river so that, needless to say, the bridge was then widened. One cannot help musing on the narrowness of a bridge which, even after its widening, seems slender by today's standards. There is a possible

The lighthouse at Start Point

70

stroll through the lovely Skaigh woods which begins from near the bridge. It was to Sticklepath that John Wesley, the eighteenth-century English preacher, first brought Methodism to Devon. He was welcomed by the large Quaker community who themselves had probably gone to the place to escape persecution elsewhere. On **Tour 8**.

Stoke Gabriel see **Tour 6**

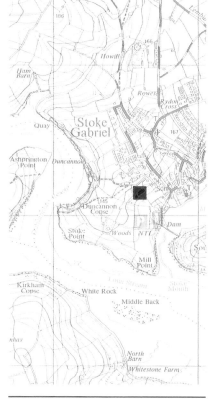

The church of St Michael and All Angels, Stokenham (above), with the unusual collection in the porch (top) of photographs of guide dogs for the blind.

dered hassock. Outside, the churchyard seems very large for a small parish and you can stroll through it on the public footpath which then takes you into the village itself. Notice the extraordinary curving chimney of the thatched part of the Tradesmans Arms public house. On **Tour 7**.

Tavistock
(191) (SX 4874)

The market town of Tavistock we see today, with its remarkable greyish green Hurdwick stone buildings, owes its origins mainly to the Russell family, the Earls and Dukes of Bedford to whom the area was passed by Henry VIII following the Dissolution in 1539. In that century, too, Sir Francis Drake was born in Tavistock and his statue may be seen at the end of Plymouth Road. The town had already had a long history and was the site of a Benedictine abbey in 974. The name of the town comes from a Saxon word meaning, apparently, 'secondary settlement by the River Tavy', the primary settlements being the two Tavy villages that were later dedicated to St Peter and St Mary. Tavistock was one of Devon's four stannary towns but, early in the 1600s, the tin was worked out, shortly to be followed, however, by the discovery of large amounts of copper ore. In Bedford Square, there is a copper statue of the nineteenth-century Duke of Bedford who developed so much of the town.

Nearby is Morwellham Quay Open Air Mu-

Stokenham
(202) (SX 8042) 6 miles E of Kingsbridge

The name of this village comes from the Saxon *Stoc-en-Hamme* which means the 'stock farm building in marshy land'. The first church here was probably built in 1186 although the oldest remaining parts of the present building, which is dedicated to St Michael and All Angels, date back to the fifteenth century. It is a fine example of a Perpendicular church, begun in the late fourteenth century, and built on the side of a hill so that its whole length can be seen from below. The original church was built by Matthew fitz Herbert, the first Lord of the Manor of Stokenham. Walk in to the porch and you will be struck by the remarkable series of photographs of guide dogs for the blind which have been donated to the church. As you go into the church itself, it is clear that it is much loved and well cared for by its parishioners — each place in the pews has its own individually hand-embroi-

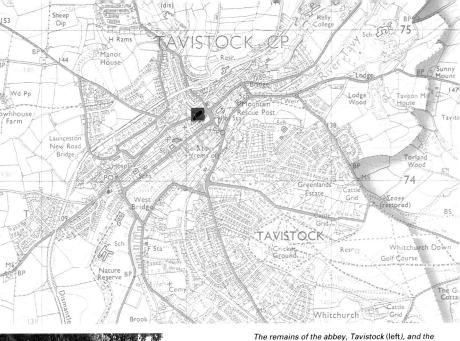

The remains of the abbey, Tavistock (left), and the stunning view over Teignmouth (right) from Shaldon, across the mouth of the River Teign.

seum, an industrial museum where visitors may ride on a riverside tramway and enter an underground copper mine as well as seeing the smithy, the cooper's workshop, or even take a carriage ride drawn by Shire horse. Tavistock is on **Tours 8** and **10**.

Teignmouth
(192) (SX 9472)
Although Teignmouth is a popular holiday resort with safe bathing everywhere but in the estuary itself, it is still a working port exporting ball clay. The older Teignmouth was lost at the hands of the French in the late seventeenth century so that the town now presents a largely elegant Georgian and Victorian face to the world. All of the usual holiday facilities are here especially in and around the grassy Den area but, for the less energetic, there is The House of Marbles & Teign Valley Glass Studios where visitors can watch glass being made by hand. Teignmouth Museum, at 29 French Street, shows how the town and harbour have developed through the

centuries. Teignmouth is on **Tour 3** and, as its name suggests, is situated on the estuary of the lovely River Teign.

Templer Way
Based on the Haytor Granite Tramway ★ and Canal, the Templer Way is a footpath which, with the aid of grants from the Countryside Commission, will link Haytor and Teignmouth ★ . Some sections are open at the time of going to press and are waymarked — a 17-mile path was opened officially in the spring of 1987. There is also a 3¹/₂-mile Heritage Trail providing a circular walk from Stover Country Park, some 3 miles south-east of Bovey Tracey ★ . The way takes its name from the Templer family whose fortune was established by James Templer in the eighteenth century from dock building. It was a descendant, George Templer, who built the granite tramway. There is a good deal to see along the Templer Way including the granite rails of the tramway itself, milestones, canal locks, and clay cellars. Features of special interest are described on information boards along the way.

Topsham
(192) (SX 9688) 4 miles SE of Exeter
No visit to this part of Devon would be complete without an exploration of the extraordinary village of Topsham, so close physically to Exeter ★ and yet so different. From the sixteenth to the nineteenth centuries, Topsham was an important port on the River Exe, catering for the thriving woollen industry of Exeter. Its links with Holland in the late seventeenth century are admirably demonstrated by the Dutch-style houses on the Strand where Topsham Museum

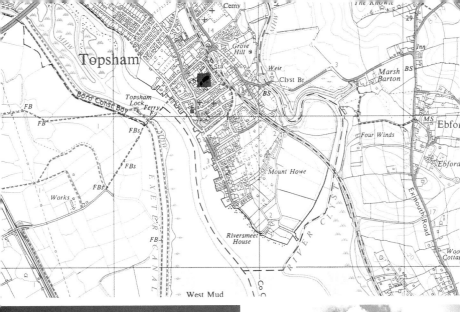

The Dutch House at Topsham (above), and two views of Trinity Church, Torbryan (above right and right).

is also situated. The museum's displays concentrate on the village's maritime past. It is open throughout the year on Monday, Wednesday, and Saturday in the afternoons. On **Tour 1**.

Torbay and Dartmouth Railway see Paignton

Torbryan

(202) (SX 8265) 4½ miles SW of Newton Abbot Torbryan hardly seems to exist at all but its church stands out immediately for one notable feature — its fine Perpendicular tower appears to have been whitewashed! In fact, it is limewash and is one of the few remaining examples of a treatment which was formerly applied to most of the churches in the region. Trinity Church was built in about 1400 and stands on the site of an earlier church which was destroyed by fire in 1360. Go inside and look at the fifteenth-century screen — it displays paintings of forty saints, some of which are very rare. The rector of Trinity Church during Puritan times was Edward Goswell and it is he who is said to have saved the paintings by having them whitewashed. There are some fine enclosed pews, too. Torbryan is on **Tour 5**.

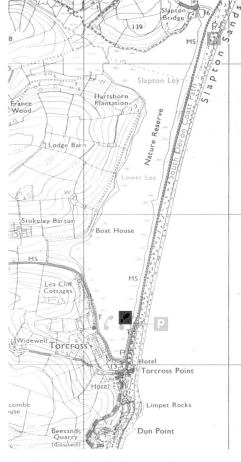

This Sherman Tank was recovered from the sea at Torcross.

Torcross

(202) (SX 8241) 7 miles SW of Dartmouth
Having survived the storms of 1979, and now boasting a new sea wall, Torcross looks set to remain an attractive fishing village caught between the sea to the east and the freshwater lagoon of Slapton Ley nature reserve at its back. The Sherman Tank in the public car park comes as something of a surprise to new visitors to the village. With the inspiration and energy of a local innkeeper, Ken Small, the tank was recovered from the sea in 1984, and set up as a permanent memorial to the 749 men who died during an amphibious landing rehearsal for D Day. The support boats were attacked by German Schnellbooten. On **Tour 6**.

Torre Abbey see Torquay

Torquay

(202) (SX 9163)
Torquay proudly describes itself as 'the jewel of the [English] Riviera with a style of its own'. Its Mediterranean affinities, along with Paignton and Brixham, stem from a climate in which palm trees and other subtropical plants are able to flourish alongside those more typical of an English countryside. On the other hand, it has also been termed 'a town built to accommodate invalids' because it is so sheltered. It is a bustling holiday resort, packed to the gunwales with hotels and guest houses, restaurants, discotheques, and nightclubs.

First granted borough status in 1891, during Victoria's reign, Torquay attracted those who could afford it to improve their health in a watering place which has one of the best cli-

mates England has to offer. Before that, Torquay had been recommended for 'bathing and summer visitors' as early as 1794 and a few years later many properties put up for sale in the area advertised their advantages by emphasizing the equable climate and the convenient sea bathing. It is in this century, however, that Torquay's popularity as a holiday resort has reached its acme, and it is continuing to develop as a conference centre and a mecca for yachtsmen, too.

Torre Abbey, Torquay.

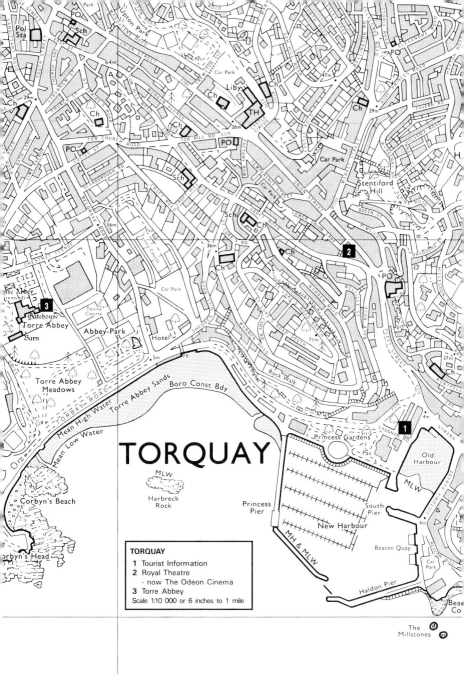

TORQUAY

1 Tourist Information
2 Royal Theatre
  - now The Odeon Cinema
3 Torre Abbey
Scale 1:10 000 or 6 inches to 1 mile

There seems to have been a theatre in Torquay as early as 1827, if not before, and a new theatre was completed some ten years later. The Royal Theatre, Torquay, as it is now known, was built in 1880, as The Theatre, largely through the driving force of a company formed by a Dr Gillow. On 8 March 1886, the then Princess of Wales visited The Theatre and it added 'Royal' to its name. In November of the same year, it was forced to close for financial reasons al-though it was opened again about a month later. In 1932 it was to close for the last time and became the Odeon Cinema, even though cinema had been in Torquay since 1909. Today, Torquay has combined its attractions and offers the 'English Riviera Centre' which is open throughout the year and has sports facilities, a swimming pool, an auditorium, and an exhibition area

With so much to offer, it is hard to pick out

The model village at Babbacombe, Torquay.

particular points of interest but the limestone caves of Kents Cavern in Wellswood, one of Europe's most important sites of its kind, are surely worth a visit; its story goes back for more than 450 000 years. So, too, is Torre Abbey in the Kings Drive, a twelfth-century monastery converted to a private house after the Dissolution. Northwards round the headland is Babbacombe Model Village where hundreds of models and figures representing the English countryside are set out among 4 acres of gardens. It even has its own unique collection of dwarf conifer trees. There is a working pottery here, as well as the Oddicombe Beach Cliff Railway. Torquay is the starting point for **Tours 5** and **6**.

Totnes
(202) (SX 8060)

Situated almost equidistant between south-east Dartmoor and the 'English Riviera' of Torquay, Paignton, and Brixham, Totnes could be said to be the perfect centre from which to enjoy a South Devon holiday. But it is far from being just a springboard for the rest of the county. There is much to see here, too, as even a short stroll through the picturesque streets quickly proves. Totnes lies at the highest navigable point of the River Dart and has, therefore, been a port of some importance. It is thought to be England's second oldest borough although, as a settlement, its history dates back to Roman times

(Roman tiles have been found beneath the streets) and before, as finds of flint tools demonstrate.

From a distance, it is the circular keep of Totnes Castle, dating from the thirteenth and fourteenth centuries, which dominates the town, but the Guildhall, built in 1553 on the site of the Old Priory, has been described as 'the most atmospheric building in Totnes' and is still the seat of the town council. The Guildhall and the accompanying Rampart Walk are open to the public most of the year. There is so much to see here, and a booklet published by Totnes Publicity Association and available from the Tourist

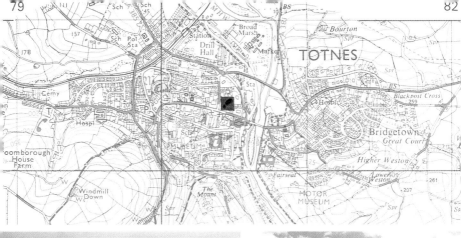

Totnes, with Bowden House (left), *the castle* (above), *and Fore Street* (below left).

Information Centre on The Plains is a mine of useful details.

No visit to Totnes would be complete, however, without a ride on one of the horse-drawn omnibuses from the Heavy Horse Centre on Steamer Quay close to the Motor Museum. Totnes Museum in Fore Street, itself built in the latter quarter of the sixteenth century as a merchant's house, is well worth a visit. At Shinner's Bridge, Dartington on the A385 road about a mile to the northwest of the town centre is the Cider Press Centre where there is a variety of craft shops. Totnes is on **Tours 5** and **6**.

Two Bridges

(191) (SX 608750) 3 miles SW of Postbridge
The clapper bridge at two Bridges is one of a number of fifteenth-century packhorse bridges which enabled travellers to journey eastwards from Tavistock. Many people think of Two Bridges as the centre of Dartmoor and the hotel here marks the increase in tourism to Dartmoor in the nineteenth century. On **Tours 4** and **8**.

Ugbrooke House

(192) (SX 8778) 1 mile SE of Chudleigh
The ancestral home of the Lords Clifford of Chudleigh, the mainly eighteenth-century Ugbrooke House is open to the public for guided tours between the end of May and August. The collection of furniture, portraits, dolls, and mili-

Weir Quay, Bere Alston

tary uniforms is superb and there is an interesting map room display. It is passed on **Tour 3**.

Vixen Tor see **Walk 11**

Weir Quay see Bere Alston

Wembury
(201) (SX 5249) 8 miles SE of Plymouth
The village of Wembury itself is a little inland from the coast and offers no great interest. St Weburgh's Church, on the other hand, is sited on the cliffs and is well worth a visit. It is thought that the church was named after a seventh-century Saxon saint, St Wereburge. The present church includes a fifteenth-century tower as well as some Norman remnants. Although he did not live here, the ancestors of the English novelist and dramatist, John Galsworthy (of *Forsyte Saga* fame) originated from the village. Wembury Beach is owned by the National Trust as is the old mill building, where there is a café during summer, just below the church. In some buildings close to the mill there is the National Trust shop. Surfing is possible from Wembury Beach at certain times of the year, and the rock pools are a treasure trove of sea creatures. On **Tour 9**.

Wheal Betsy
(191) (SX 512813) 5 miles NE of Tavistock
Owned by the National Trust, and clearly visibly from the A386 road near to the village of Mary Tavy, Wheal Betsy is the best surviving example on Dartmoor of an engine house once used in lead and silver mining. On **Tour 8**.

Widecombe-in-the-Moor
(191) (SX 7176) 7 miles W of Bovey Tracey
Few people, even if they have never visited Dartmoor, will not have heard of Widecombe even though its population is hardly more than 200 souls. It is in the song, when Uncle Tom Cobley led his grey mare to the Fair, that the village has achieved fame. Widecombe Fair is still held here on the second Tuesday of September and is known to have taken place in 1850. Despite the village's humble proportions,

Left: *The road bridge at Two Bridges.*
Below left: *Ugbrooke House.*
Below: *Vixen Tor.*

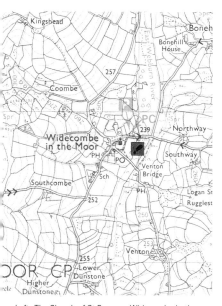

Left: *The Church of St Pancras, Widecombe-in-the-Moor.*
Below: *The tiny relict oakwood of Wistman's Wood.*

the Church of St Pancras is very grand. The present building dates from the fourteenth century although it was enlarged and the tower added in the 1500s thanks to the wealth of the local tinners. It has been referred to as the 'cathedral of the moor'.

The Old Inn was built in the fourteenth century and, although it suffered in a fire in the 1970s, much of the stonework survived — it is reputed to be haunted by a man called Harry and by the eighteenth-century Mary Tay who hanged herself when she became pregnant by a local farm worker.

The National Trust shop and Information Centre is housed in what is now called the Church House although it was orginally built as a brew house in the first half of the sixteenth century. It then became a school and is now the village hall. On **Tour 4**.

Wistman's Wood

(191) (SX 613773) 3 miles NW of Princetown
In a narrow cleft of the Devonport Leat lies the tiny relict oakwood of Wistman's Wood. With its gnarled little trees and lichen- and moss- clad branches, the wood is like something out of a fairy story and is well worth the walk along the footpath from the B3212 near the Powder Mills to find it.

Driving in South Devon and Dartmoor

Traffic permitting, with today's fast cars and high-speed motorways, it is an easy matter to cover a distance of 60 or 70 miles in an hour. This is the length of the longer of the tours described in this book but, under no circumstances, could you complete one tour within an hour — and who would want to? Even if you choose not to stop to explore the towns and villages along the way or take in one or more of the Miniwalks that have been included, you should allow yourself plenty of time. And make sure that you start out with a full tank of petrol — in Devon's more rural parts, filling stations are few and far between!

Until comparatively recently, even the main arterial roads through Devon were single carriageway roads and, although the M5 now reaches Exeter where it links up with the A38 and A30 trunk roads, many of the 'A' roads in the county are surprisingly narrow and twisting. Indeed, it is not so long ago that some farming communities near isolated but locally important towns, such as Chagford, saw their first wheeled transport!

Devon is justly famous for its sunken, flower-lined lanes; in spring, when the scent of primroses can be discerned even from a motor car, they are a sheer delight to drive along or to walk through but, in the height of the tourist season, even a comparatively light traffic load can bring you grinding to a frustrating halt. Choose your times carefully for undertaking the tours in this book and be prepared to reverse into passing places to allow on-coming traffic to pass. Most importantly, remember that, while you may only be visiting Devon for two or three weeks in a year, for the local people, and especially the farmers, these picturesque lanes are their only means of road communication and they depend on them all year. In the summer, when you are relaxing, they still have to work, so if you find yourself stuck behind a tractor, be patient. Generally, Devon drivers are very polite and go out of their way to allow you to pass.

While Devon's climate is mild, and its people welcoming, some of its roads can test the skills of the most experienced driver. The narrower byways and bridges were not constructed with motor vehicles in mind so you may find yourself having to undertake some slick manoeuvring to negotiate the more tortuous corners, hills, and junctions. And where at the beginning of a tour, the advice is that it is not for the nervous driver or for cars towing caravans, it is worth heeding the warning. The drives are intended to be enjoyed and to give a taste of the richness of South Devon and Dartmoor's highways and byways — there is little point in ruining a day by getting a caravan stuck half way across a narrow bridge!

Below: *the narrow road with passing places at Mill Bay Cove, near Salcombe, and* (right), *the narrow bridge at Postbridge.*

Tour 1
East Devon

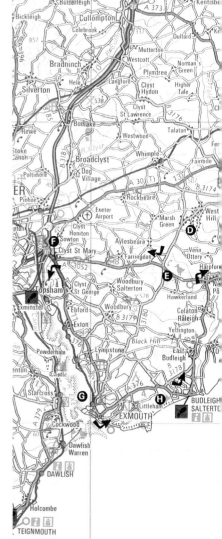

60 miles. The purpose of this tour is to show that East Devon has a great deal to offer. While the landscape may not be so dramatic as it is further west, it is pleasing to the eye and there are seaside towns to tempt children as well as at least one authentic fishing village. It is of necessity a long tour and you should allow plenty of time to enjoy it and the various strolls which are possible. Cyclists may find this tour a little too demanding to accomplish in one day.

Starting from the town centre of Axminster ★, follow the A35 towards Honiton ★. Cross over the River Axe. You then cross the River Yarty. It is possible to make a short diversion to the extraordinary little village of Shute ★ by turning left on to the Shute Road (**A**) by a World War I memorial cross some 1¾ miles out of Axminster. To continue the tour, carry on along the A35 and drive through the village of Wilmington.

The road descends into Honiton on a twisting route. Turn left at the first mini-roundabout into the town — you can follow the main street unless you wish to use the bypass. About 400 yards the other side of the town, turn left on the A375 (**B**) as though heading towards Sidmouth ★ and Budleigh Salterton ★. Take the first exit at the mini-roundabout.

Turn right towards Ottery St Mary ★ on to the B3174 by the Hare and Hounds pub (**C**). A 1 in 5 hill descends and twists, and in the distance, you can see Ottery. At the T-junction, bear right signposted to Exeter ★. Continue through the town following the one-way system. Go over the road bridge across the River Otter. Turn left on to the B3177 towards Exmouth ★ off the B3174 towards Exeter. Then, just the other side of West Hill continue bearing left on to the B3180 (**D**). By the Halfway Inn (**E**), turn right on to the A3052 to Clyst St Mary. The tour bypasses the village itself although it may be worth stopping here if only to look at the extraordinary painting on the outside wall of the Half Moon pub.

Continuing on the A3052 towards Exeter, drive down the hill to the roundabout and go straight across following the AA HR route signs. Continue on the A376 and, just before reaching the roundabout with the M5, turn left (**F**) on to a small road, signposted to Topsham ★ and the Blue Ball Inn. As you approach Topsham,

at the first T-junction, turn left to continue on the tour or right and then left past the station to park in the free car park for a stroll around this delightful village.

To carry on with the tour, pass the Bridge Inn on the left, and cross the River Clyst. At the mini-roundabout, by the George and Dragon pub, turn right on to the A376. Pass through Exton. A short diversion from the main part of the tour will take you into the Exe-side village of Lympstone. Narrow passages lead down to the river between leaning buildings which seem almost to be tumbling into the river. Don't bring the car into the village but park in the free car park. Just beyond the turning to Lympstone, on the busy A376, is the Roundhouse or À la Ronde ★.

Continue on to Exmouth (**G**) on the A376. Take the first exit left at the mini-roundabout signposted towards Budleigh

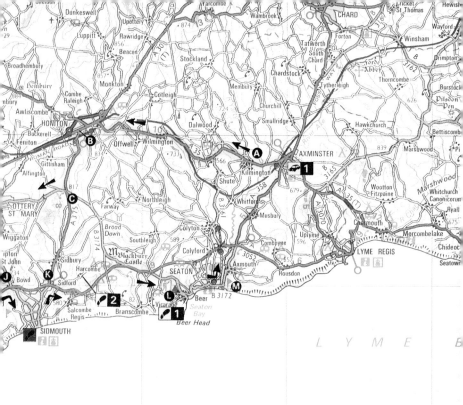

Scale 1:250 000 or ¼ INCH to 1 MILE

Salterton. After the traffic lights bear immediately right to Budleigh Salterton, then left. Continue straight on up the hill. It is possible either to take advantage of Exmouth's resort facilities or to look around the town. At the next roundabout, take the first exit left signposted 'Budleigh Salterton 5', and then go straight on at the next mini-roundabout.

The A376 winds and undulates towards Budleigh Salterton. Before the village of Knowle, cross the dismantled railway line, go around a sharp right-hand bend, and carry on to Budleigh Salterton (**H**). Here, you can either follow the road down to the sea front and along the strand, doubling back to pick up A376 again, or you can turn left . If you have time on this rather long tour, you may find that a stroll along the strand and into the town is relaxing.

The A376 road now follows the west bank of the River Otter through East Budleigh to Collaton Raleigh and then to Newton Poppleford, but here again, a short diversion to East Budleigh and Hayes Barton ★, the home of Sir Walter Raleigh, is worth the effort. And, soon after, yet another short diversion could take you across the river to Otterton.

Pass through Colaton Raleigh and carry on to Newton Poppleford where, at the T-junction with the Exeter Road, turn right signposted to Lyme Regis, Seaton ★, and

Sidmouth. Pass over the bridge spanning the River Otter and continue on the A376. About a mile beyond Newton Poppleford turn right to Sidmouth on the B3176 (**J**) where you could stop for a stroll.

For those continuing with the tour, turn left just before reaching the end of the strand where there is a large car park. Cross the ford over the Otter and join the A3052 or stay on the west bank of the Otter and make your way back to the main road that way. Turn right on to the A3052 (**K**) and cross the River Sid. Just past the river is the left-hand turning which leads to the start of **Walk 2**. About 4 miles beyond the junction between the A375 Honiton road and the A3052, turn right on to the B3174 towards Beer ★. If you decide to take a stroll around Beer village centre, cross the road and follow the signposts. **Walk 1** is from Beer.

Alternatively, turn left to Seaton as directed (**L**). Follow the signposted routed down to the sea front where there are car parks. Drive along the sea-front strand to the end where the road then bears left. Turn right at the T-junction. Cross the little road bridge over the Axe (**M**) and follow the road up the estuary along its east bank. Continue on the B3172, through Axmouth, as though heading towards Lyme Regis. Turn right and immediately left, and return to Axminster.

85

Tour 2
North of Dartmoor

40 miles. Although this is a comparatively short tour, it does give you the chance to explore two North Dartmoor towns of some importance, as well as the extraordinary Castle Drogo designed by Edwin Lutyens. And the return route offers good views across attractive mid-Devon farmland to the moor further south. Cyclists may find that this part of the tour is too busy to be really enjoyable during the height of the season.

Leave Exeter ★ on the B3212 towards Moretonhampstead ★. Continue along the road and, at Long Down, the countryside opens out into fine rolling and wooded country almost resembling downland. Follow the signs for Dunsford and Moretonhampstead. Soon there are splendid views ahead from this part of the route. Although the road is generally of good quality and it is, unlike many of the lanes these tours include, proper two carriageway, there are some deceptively sharp corners on it so it is as well to drive with care. It is worth noting, too, that it is still possible to purchase real farmhouse cider from farms along the roadside.

You soon enter Dartmoor National Park again near the village of Dunsford ★ (**A**). Go over Steps Bridge, where there is a possible stroll, and follow the attractive wooded river valley on a valley-side road with quite a steep drop to the right. Gradually, the valley becomes less severe. Pass through the village of Doccombe and go straight on at the next crossroads continuing towards Moretonhampstead. As you descend the hill, there are lovely views of the patchwork fields of red and green with the moor behind. Approaching the town of Moretonhampstead, at the stop sign by the White Hart where there is a cross roads, turn right (**B**) signposted to Okehampton ★ and Chagford ★ .(You may wish to interrupt the tour to stroll around Moretonhampstead which has some interesting buildings.) Then turn immediately left by Moreton House. At Chagford Cross continue straight on towards Chagford. In the next little village, turn left (**C**), signposted to Chagford, opposite the Easton Court Hotel and restaurant. You will soon see Chagford Church on the hill ahead above the village. Continue on to Chagford centre where there is a car park. Chagford is an ancient stannary town dating from the early fourteenth century and is well worth strolling around.

Leave Chagford by the Okehampton/ Moretonhampstead road by which you came into the town. About ½ mile from the town centre, fork left (**D**) signposted to the swimming pool. Go over the narrow stone bridge which crosses the still young River Teign. From here the remarkable twentieth-century Castle Drogo ★ can just be seen on the hill ahead to the right. You then come to a crossroads with the A382 at the Sandy Park Inn. Go straight across on to the minor road signposted to Drewsteignton ★ , Castle Drogo, and Fingle Bridge. This is an awkward junction and caution is needed. Castle Drogo can now be seen clearly on the hill to the right. By any standards it is a remarkable-looking building, especially when you bear in mind how recently it was built. It does resemble

The Drew Arms, a wonderful old world pub, where you can literally help yourself to drinks!

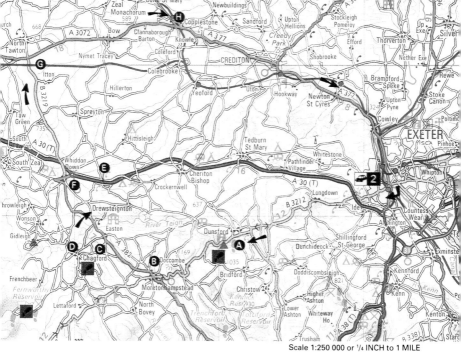

Scale 1:250 000 or ¼ INCH to 1 MILE

for all the world a medieval castle. Continue on past Castle Drogo bearing right towards Drewsteignton and Fingle Bridge at Trennaway Cross. As is so often the case on these tours, this is a narrow road with passing places.

Just past the village sign announcing Drewsteignton, bear left signposted towards Crockernwell and Exeter — straight on will take you to Fingle Bridge. Carry on, passing the village square where the Drew Arms, a wonderful old world pub, can be seen to the right. Alternatively, park in the square and call in for a pint of real ale or cider. Honesty is the key word here for you can help yourself to drinks and just leave your money on the kitchen table — there is no bar. Continue towards Crockernwell and Exeter at Netherton Cross and, at the next fork, bear left along the unsignposted route — this is Veet Mill Cross. At the T-junction turn left, again unsignposted, and at the next T-junction, turn left heading towards Whiddon Down. There are pleasant views in most directions from this road which, it must be admitted, is unusual in much of Devon because of the sunken nature of many of the lanes. Cross over the A30 trunk road (**E**), and your route runs parallel to the A30 towards Whiddon Down for about 3 miles.

At the roundabout where your road crosses the A30 (**F**), continue straight over towards Moretonhampstead, Weekly, Torrington, South Zeal, Sticklepath ★, and North Tawton. This is the A382 joining the B3219. Just after the Whiddon Down town sign, opposite the Post Inn, turn right on to the B3219 signposted to Winkly, Torrington, Bude, Sprayton, and North Tawton. Cross over the A30 again, this time on a flyover, and carry straight on signposted to North Tawton. At the bottom of the hill pass under the railway line and, at the next junction about a mile before you get to North Tawton, turn right on to the A3072 (**G**) towards Crediton ★. You are now driving through open farming country where there is a patchwork of red and green of the ploughed fields and fields under crops. Carry on through the small town of Bow. In Copplestone, bear right on to the A377 signposted to Exeter (**H**). This is at a T-junction and it is also signposted to Crediton and Tiverton. Go over the railway line. There are fine views to the right with farmland in the foreground and the moor on the far horizon. Although this is a main A road, it makes for pleasant travelling because of the views, and the route gives a good impression of this part of central Devon.

Continue on through the main street of Crediton (or stop for a stroll around the town, especially to explore the one remaining historic building — the very grand church) and, just beyond the church, fork right towards Exeter on the A377. Continue through Newton St Cyres and pass through the village of Half Moon which, as one drives at least, seems rather less attractive than its name might suggest. Cross the River Yeo and you are back in the outskirts of the city of Exeter, turning right at the next roundabout, still on the A377, to the city centre.

87

Tour 3
A Tour of Two Rivers

40 miles. It is always surprising how soon after leaving such a large and busy city as Exeter, it is possible to be in delightful rural Devon. This tour gives you a chance to appraise the popular resorts of Teignmouth and Dawlish as well as to visit such interesting attractions as the Brunel Atmospheric Railway Pumping House or Powderham Castle. There are one or two places where the roads are narrow, twisting, and steep. Cyclists may have to push their bikes on these stretches.

Leave Exeter ★ on the B3212 to Dunsford ★ and Moretonhampstead ★ . About a mile after crossing the River Exe, just before a turning to the Pathfinder Village, turn left on a minor road (**A**) to Ide going under the A30 trunk road which links with the M5 motorway. This turning is not always easy to notice so you will need to look carefully for it. Continue through the village of Ide, past the pub, and on up the hill. Bear left at the fork towards Dunchideock and, at the next crossroads, go straight on to Dunchideock. Ahead a tower on a hill can be seen — could this be a folly? Dunchideock nestles in a pleasant valley.

Just after the Dunchideock village sign, turn right (**B**) towards Doddiscombsleigh. Soon after, look out for a plaque on the wall of a thatched building carrying the unusual sign 'W Drake Licensed to Sell Tobacco'. Continue on up a narrow lane where, through breaks in the hedges, there are glimpses of rich farmland. At Willhayes Cross, go straight over to Doddiscombsleigh but, as you go down the hill, the electricity pylon rather mars the view ahead. At the Doddiscombsleigh village sign, bear left. At the T-junction turn right towards Christow. Then, at the fork, go left towards Ashton past the Nobody Inn. Drive through a pleasant valley where the cuttings are deep and their sides steep. Some of the descents and ascents on the road are rather dramatic. Turn right at the next T-junction, passing the Manor Inn, and go over the little stone bridge to arrive at the B3193 (**C**). Turn left towards Chudleigh ★ .

Pass the turning for Canonteign Falls ★ to the right and, shortly after, turn right (**D**) on to an unsignposted road more or less opposite a rock face on the other side of the road. Go over another little bridge and drive up the hill. This road needs first-gear driving for most cars. At the T-junction, turn right towards Hennock. At the top of the hill, just in front of some council houses, turn left towards Bovey Tracey ★ (which is

Scale 1:250 000 or ¼ INCH to 1 MILE

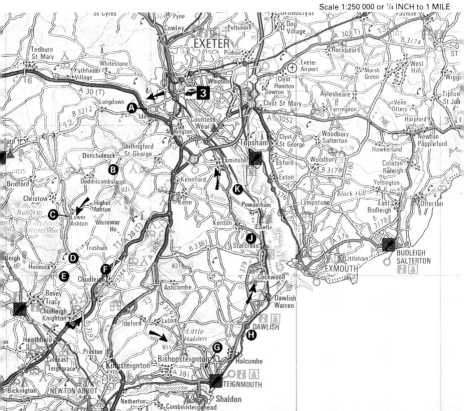

also visited on **Tour 4**) and Chudleigh Knighton. Bear left down the hill towards Bovey and, as you descend, lovely views open up ahead. Follow the signs to Bovey Tracey and, at the next junction, fork right at Little Helstonsbench Cross. To continue the tour, turn left at the T-junction (**E**) or, if you want to stroll around the town, turn right into Bovey (pronounced 'Buvvy') Tracey.

Out of Bovey Tracey, take the B3344 towards Chudleigh Knighton. Shortly after leaving Bovey, the road becomes attractively gorse lined as you approach Chudleigh Knighton. Turn left at the T-junction in Chudleigh Knighton and continue straight on at the next junction towards Chudleigh, still on the B3344. For a short distance the road runs parallel to the A38 trunk road. Pass Silverlands Model World and Chudleigh Motor Museum. Go straight across the A38 on a flyover and, very soon, enter the ancient wool town of Chudleigh. It is now largely a nineteenth- and twentieth-century creation because more than 60 per cent of the old town was burnt down in a fire in 1807.

In the centre of Chudleigh, turn right (**F**) signposted to Ugbrooke House ★ , going through the narrow backstreets of Chudleigh. Go over the little stone bridge and continue straight on up Mount Pleasant. Continue up on the winding lane turning round to the right at Biddlecombe Cross signposted to Ideford, Teignmouth ★ , and Ugbrooke. This is a pleasant tree-lined road. Pass Ugbrooke House and go under the A38, signposted to Torquay ★ this time, and then Ideford and Luton. Pass under the stone bridge and, at the T-junction, turn left signposted to Ideford and Luton. Drive through the village of Ideford, bearing right at the fork towards Luton and Teignmouth — this is effectively straight on. At the right junction, turn left towards Luton, Haldon, and Teignmouth, and bear right at the next corner. Ahead is Haldon Moor with patchwork red and green fields in the foreground.

Continue through the village of Luton and carry straight on towards Haldon and Teignmouth. You are now driving along another narrow lane with passing places, climbing up towards Haldon Moor. Ignore the left turning to Exeter and carry straight on to Haldon and Teignmouth. At the crossroads, marked Exeter to the left and Kingsteignton and Bishopsteignton to the right, go straight across passing Teignmouth Golf Club practice area. Here there is a good view to the sea. At the T-junction, turn right on to the B3192 Teignmouth Road and follow the long

Listed as a building of outstanding architectural and historic merit, St Clements Church, Powderham was built in 1258.

descent down into Teignmouth itself. (Teignmouth is also passed on **Tour 5.**) Nearing the bottom of the hill, at the traffic lights, turn left (**G**) towards the town centre and Dawlish ★ .

At the next roundabout, continue the tour straight on to Dawlish or turn right into the town centre to explore the dual nature of this popular holiday resort and stroll along the promenade. Pass the rather attractive station and follow the one-way system towards Dawlish. Continuing on through Dawlish, and with the splendid railway station to the right, turn right (**H**) towards Dawlish Warren and the golf club about ³/₄ mile out of the town. The road stretches ahead parallel to the railway line and you pass through Cockwood. At the T-junction by the little harbour turn right on the A379 and pass the Brunel Atmospheric Pumping House and Railway ★ .

About ¹/₂ mile past the pumping house, turn right (**J**) in front of a large house on an unsignposted road. You pass St Clements Church of Powderham ★. This is a red breccia church from the Old Red Sandstone. It was built in 1258 and is listed as a building of outstanding architectural and historic merit. The doors at the west end of the church are thought to be the doors of the original rood screen. The font is also original. The supporting columns in the nave appear to lean outwards from their centre. Pass the entrance to Powderham Castle a little way beyond the church and, shortly after, look in the fields to the right where there is a little house with a lovely round end. At the T-junction (**K**) turn right on to the A379 signposted to Exeter.

Tour 4
Eastern Dartmoor and the 'In Country'

48 miles. You should allow plenty of time for this tour because there is much to see and some of the roads are very narrow, steep, and winding. Indeed, you should certainly not attempt it in icy weather during winter, or if you are towing a caravan for you will surely get stuck on at least one of the narrow bridges or bends. Cyclists must be fit to complete this in a day although it would be a splendid ride.

Start the tour from the free car park in the one-way street of Station Road, Buckfastleigh ★ . Turn right out of the car park and then left on to the Dartbridge Road (**A**) towards Buckfast Abbey ★ . Just before reaching the A38, you could make a short diversion to the left on the Old Buckfast Road to stroll around Buckfast Abbey .

Continue the tour by taking the next left turn signposted to Ashburton ★ and Princetown ★ just before the main junction with the A38. At the T-junction turn left towards Ashburton and Two Bridges, and then immediately right towards Ashburton, Widecombe ★ , and Buckland-in-the-Moor ★ . Continue through the town centre of Ashburton, and carry straight on ignoring the left turn to Widecombe. Just the other side of the town, fork left signposted A38 to Exeter and, in about ½ mile, rejoin the A38 (**B**).

After approximately 4 miles, take the A382 signposted to Bovey Tracey ★, Moretonhampstead ★ , and Newton Abbot ★ at Drumbridges (**C**). Then take the second exit at the roundabout towards Bovey Tracey and Moretonhampstead. The first exit from this roundabout is signposted to 'Miniature Railway Park 1¼'. At the first roundabout before Bovey Tracey go straight on towards the town centre on A382. At the next roundabout, continue the tour straight on towards Moretonhampstead or turn right for a stroll around this delightful, honest working town (Bovey Tracey is also featured on **Tour 3**).

Continuing on the tour, cross the River Bovey and go past the first marked road to the left; the road goes through a kind of chicane. Immediately after, turn left (**D**) on to a very narrow minor road with passing places where there is room only for one car. The road descends steeply and becomes a truly delightful Devon lane. When you come to a fork in the road, turn left on an unsignposted road between the remains of a bridge which once carried the railway. Then turn immediately right to Lustleigh ★ and continue along a narrow lane with wooded hills to the right and the lovely River Bovey flowing on the left. Pass under another stone bridge and, at the next T-junction bear right, effectively straight on, signposted to Lustleigh and Moretonhampstead.

Turn left at the next T-junction signposted to Lustleigh and then cross the river and the line of the disused railway once again. Although the signpost suggests that Lustleigh is further on, you have already travelled through part of the village. Follow the road round to the left, still signposted to Lustleigh. Caseley is signposted to the right and, about 100 yards further on just before reaching Lustleigh church, turn right on to a road which is indicated as being 'unsuitable for lorries'. The route climbs steeply along a tree-lined sunken lane. At Sanduck (**E**), past the farm buildings on the right-hand side of the road, there is a stone cross. The road turns sharply left. Continue on towards North Bovey and Moretonhampstead ignoring a turning to the left.

At the next junction, which is not signposted, turn left. Follow the winding, descending road through high-banked hedges. Cross the rivers on two very narrow bridges which are not suitable for caravans (or even very wide cars!). Do not take the first turning signposted to Manaton ★ , but continue straight on up the hill. Turn left at a T-junction and wind on up the hill again, eventually emerging on to the B3344 where you turn left, signposted to Manaton and Becka Falls ★ .

At the crossroads in Manaton, go straight across, continuing straight on at the next crossroads passing the pub and the post office. In about ⅓ of a mile, you can continue the tour by forking right on to an unsignposted road. Alternatively, carry on, cross the little stream and in about 200 yards you will come to the car park of Becka Falls which is well worth a stroll. Turn right (**F**) to continue the tour on another minor road which is signposted to Beckaford (**Walk 7** passes this way) only from the opposite direction. Cross another very narrow stone bridge taking care of your wheels. Just before Haytor ★ Vale, turn right on to the B3387 road between Widecombe and Bovey Tracey. Haytor Rocks can now clearly be seen on the right. Carry straight on past the first car park, heading towards Widecombe and park in the next car park for a stroll up to Haytor Rocks.

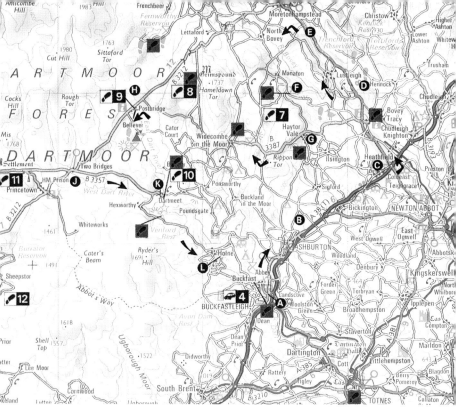

Scale 1:250 000 or ¼ INCH to 1 MILE

Go over a cattle grid and bear right towards Widecombe (**G**). It is now a 1 in 5 descent from the moorland plateau down to Widecombe. Although Widecombe is more tourist-oriented than perhaps 'Uncle Tom Cobley' would have liked, it is still worth stopping for a stroll or refreshment at the Old Inn. Continue past the church and follow the signs to Postbridge. At the next left-hand turning, bear right and continue as signposted. Go right at the next turning signposted to Postbridge, Princetown ★ , and Moretonhampstead and right again at the next junction. Continue straight on across the next crossroads and, where the road then turns left, go straight on to Postbridge.

At the next junction turn left towards Princetown and Postbridge, and then cross a stream. You will see a large forested area ahead and to the left. Do not be tempted to turn right at the next junction. Cross another stone bridge and, eventually, you will emerge on to the B3212 at Postbridge (**H**) where you turn left towards Two Bridges ★ and Princetown. It is worth parking here if only to stroll up to the splendid clapper bridge or take in the excellent Information Centre. This is also the starting point for **Walk 9** and is included on **Tour 8**.

Drive on in a south-westerly direction along the B3212 and, at Two Bridges (**J**)

take the B3357 left back towards Dartmeet ★ . Cross the West Dart river. Wind down towards the popular beauty spot of Dartmeet (**K**), so called because the East and West Dart rivers come together here. If you wish to park in the large free car park, and take a stroll around, there is plenty to enjoy here. **Walk 10** starts from the car park at Dartmeet.

From the car park turn back right up the hill and over the bridge, and take the minor road to Hexworthy almost at the top of the hill. The road now follows the river and continues down across another narrow stone bridge. From Hexworthy a steep hill ascends at an incline of 1 in 4 on the narrow road. Turn left as you reach the Forest Inn, and the road zig-zags steeply upwards. Bear left, signposted to Holne ★. Go over another little bridge up to Combe's Tor where there is parking and scope for strolls or longer walks to look at stone circles and hut circles. Pass Venford Reservoir and continue on to Holne, following the road round to the left. At the next junction, take the right turn signposted to Holne and Buckfastleigh. Ignore the next left turn immediately after. There is free parking in Holne (**L**) turning right just past the Church House Inn. Continue down the hill following the signposts to Buckfastleigh. Where the 30 mph sign appears, turn right.

91

Tour 5
Torquay, Newton Abbot, and Dartington

36 miles. This is the shortest of all the tours in the book but it does give you the chance to take in some of the main tourist attractions of Torquay on the way. Perhaps, though, it is more noteworthy for the interesting little villages of Denbury and Torbryan. It is not difficult to stray from the route if the instructions are not followed carefully but you may, in any case, wish to create your own alternatives.

From the Beacon Quay car park in Torquay ★, turn right out of the entrance and drive up the hill, passing the Imperial Hotel. Bear left, signposted to Daddyhole Plain and Meadfoot Beach, and continue straight on without turning right to Daddyhole Plain unless you wish to take a stroll at the viewpoint. Turn right at the T junction with Meadfoot Road. Descending the hill, rocky islands can be seen in the bay, of which the largest is Thatcher Rock. Continue straight on, signposted to Babbacombe, on the Ilsham Road. Just past Kent's Cavern turn right, signposted to Babbacombe, Newton Abbot ★, and Teignmouth ★. At the T-junction with the Babbacombe Road, turn right and pass the Palace Hotel on the right. Just past the hotel there is a possible short detour to Anstey's Cove to the right where there is a car park and a possible stroll along the cliff between Hope's Nose and Anstey's Cove. You will need to follow the one-way system to rejoin the tour near Kent's Cavern again.

By the Rose Grange Hotel past Perinville Road on the left, turn right, signposted to the beaches and downs. There is a car park immediately on the right and it is possible to drive down to Babbacombe beach (**A**). Alternatively, simply drive along the coast road which enjoys attractive sea views. Shortly after, there is Oddicombe Cliff Railway down to the beach. Turn right at the next T-junction (**B**) and continue straight on, signposted to Teignmouth and Newton Abbot. At the mini-roundabout, turn left and follow the one-way system, bearing right past the Crown and Sceptre pub. Then, there is a give way at which you go straight on down the hill. At the T-junction at the bottom of the hill, turn right signposted to Teignmouth. Pass the imposing building of Brunel Manor, a business and conference centre. If you wish, you could make the detour to the right on a narrow one-way road down to Maidencombe village where there is car parking and a possible stroll down to the beach. To return to the tour, follow the one-way system back to the main road.

Continue down through Shaldon, where there is a wildlife collection, towards the Teign estuary. Turn left towards Teignmouth and Dawlish ★ (both visited on Tour 3) on the A379. Cross the Teign and turn left at the T-junction on to the A381 towards Kingsteignton and Newton Abbot (**C**). Go straight across the roundabout signposted to Kingsteignton on the B3193. At the next small roundabout, turn right towards Kingsteignton again and, at the mini-roundabout, turn left towards Newton Abbot. At yet another mini-roundabout, continue on towards Newton Abbot. At the next mini-roundabout, by a superstore, continue straight on, passing the Newton Abbot racecourse on the left. Go over the railway and, at the roundabout, carry straight on towards the town centre. At the clock tower (**D**), go straight ahead towards Totnes ★, and straight on again at the mini-roundabout.

A little way out of the town, at the mini-roundabout, head towards Ogwell and Denbury ★. At the crossroads, go straight on towards Denbury and Woodland. Follow the signs towards Denbury. Unless you plan to visit the village (well worth a short stroll), turn left towards Torbryan ★ just before you get to Denbury. At the next crossroads, turn left towards Torbryan and Ipplepen, then turn right at the next junction towards Torbryan. This is a narrow road with a poor surface. Go on down into Torbryan where the splendid church has a lime-washed tower (**E**).

Fork right just outside the village up an unmarked lane, and then turn right again signposted to Broadhempston at Well Barn Cross. At Pool Cross, continue on round to the right towards Broadhempston and drive into the village. Passing the village sign, continue straight on signposted to Broadhempston and Woodland. Shortly after, turn left. Having driven through the village of Broadhempston, at the T-junction, turn right signposted to Buckfastleigh ★, Lands Cove, Woodland, and Ashburton ★. Turn left in front of Church Hill Cottages, passing the Monks Retreat Public House and carry on towards Buckfastleigh. Ignore the left turning towards Staverton and Totnes, and carry straight on towards Lands Cove and Buckfastleigh. Ignore the right turning to Woodland and Denbury and follow the road signposted, in this case, to Staver-

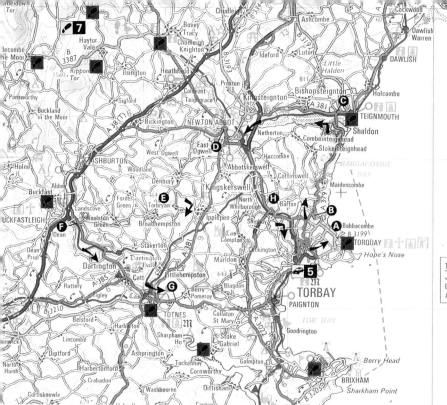

Scale 1:250 000 or ¼ INCH to 1 MILE

ton. Go over a little stone bridge and continue straight on, this time indicated to Buckfastleigh and Ashburton. At Memory Cross, go straight across towards Buckfastleigh and, at the next T-junction, turn right signposted to Ashburton and Buckfastleigh.

Ignore unmarked junctions to right and left and descend through attractive woodland over a little stream and up out the other side of the valley into open farmland with a coniferous forest on the right. At Higherbeara Cross, turn left signposted to Totnes and Buckfastleigh. Go down an attractive wildflower-lined lane in a pleasant open valley. Turn left at the T-junction signposted to Dartington and Totnes (**F**). You are now on the A384 beside the line of the Dart Valley Steam Railway. Cross the River Dart over Riverford Bridge. Approaching Dartington, at the next crossroads, turn left for a short detour to Dartington Hall ★ or continue on the tour. If you take the detour, you will pass the rather distinctive looking house on the right which was designed by Edwin Lutyens. Stroll around the grounds of Dartington Hall.

Continue on to Totnes, passing the old mill building with its undershot mill wheel. Continue on the A385 Paignton Road over the railway bridge and past the station. Totnes is an attractive town and it is worth

stopping for a stroll if you have time. At the next roundabout, take the first main exit signposted to Paignton and Newton Abbot. Go over the River Dart and, at the next roundabout, bear right towards Paignton. Then bear left (**G**) to Berry Pomeroy and go through the village towards Berry Pomeroy Castle ★, ignoring the next left to Berry Castle unless you intend to visit it. Continue on signposted to Marldon. At the next crossroads, go straight on towards Marldon at Glazegate Cross. At Marldon Cross, carry straight on and, at the first mini-roundabout, turn left, then left again at the second mini-roundabout down Vicarage Hill. At the crossroads carry straight on towards Compton along another narrow road with passing places. At the first T-junction past Compton Castle ★, turn right signposted to North Whilborough. At the next fork, where there is only a signpost from the direction you have come, turn right and go into the village of North Whilborough, or Wilborough as it was spelt previously.

At the first T-junction, turn right and then right again at the next T-junction. Turn left towards South Whilborough and wind through the village on a very rough road. Turn right at the T-junction on to a slightly more major minor road. Turn right back (**H**) into Torquay on the Newton Road — this is a very difficult junction.

Tour 6
Torquay and the Dart Estuary

44 miles. This is an opportunity to explore some of the little villages on either side of the Dart Estuary as well as to visit Slapton Ley Nature reserve. From Slapton, a short drive along the coast takes you to the west bank of the Dart at Dartmouth and a trip across one of the ferries — the lower ferry is recommended for this tour.

Leave Torquay ★ on the coast road (A379) towards Paignton ★ . As you approach Paignton, stay in the right-hand lane for the town centre and Totnes ★ . Bear left and then immediately right towards the town centre and Totnes. Continue following the signs for Totnes and the town centre, turning right at the end of Eugene Road and then left at the next T-junction at the end of Paris Road. Turn right on to the (A385) towards Totnes into Cecil Road (**A**). Pass the sign for Kirkham House. At the mini-roundabout, carry straight on up the hill and down the other side. This is Colley End Road. Turn left at the give way and, at the crossroads with traffic lights, continue straight on towards Brixham on the A3022. After rather more than a mile past the traffic lights, turn right at the next T-junction and then right to Galmpton (**B**) immediately after the traffic lights and T-junction turning into Langdon Lane.

Go over the mini-roundabout, turning right at the bottom towards Stoke Gabriel. Go up the twisting, 1 in 5 hill and down again. At the first right turning, go on to Stoke Gabriel, passing a large stone barn. Continue on towards the village centre, then turn left at Four Cross and drive into Stoke Gabriel. Carry on down towards the River Dart where there is a possible stroll by the river.

Drive back out of the village and turn left on to the road signposted to Aish. At the next T-junction, turn left, signposted to Aish and Totnes. This is another narrow road with passing places. Just past the Hamlet of Aish, bear right by the 'No Through Road' sign. Avoid turnings to right and left, and then turn left at the T-junction just past the garage, signposted to Totnes ★ . Follow the road signposted to Plymouth ★ and Newton Abbot ★ and, at the first roundabout, take the Kingsbridge ★ , Buckfastleigh ★ , Plymouth, Exeter ★ , exit unless you plan to visit the historic town of Totnes which is also visited on **Tour 5**. Cross the River Dart

by the Brutus Bridge and continue following the main routes through Totnes. At the traffic lights turn left towards Kingsbridge, Dartmouth ★ , and Avonwick on to the A381. At the next lights carry on following the signs to Dartmouth, Kingsbridge, and this time Salcombe ★ .

Take the next left to Ashprington, Tuckenhay, and Cornworthy (**C**). Follow the signs for Ashprington, Bow Bridge and Cornworthy, and Bowden House ★ . Continue on the tour and, at the crossroads, go straight on towards Ashprington, also signposted to Bow Bridge, Tuckenhay, and Cornworthy. Drop down into the village of Ashprington and turn right at the cross in the centre of the village. At the T-junction turn left to Tuckenhay and Cornworthy and go over Bow Bridge at Bow Bridge Cross. Bear left over the bridge past the front of the Waterman's Arms. Drive through the riverside village of Tuckenhay where you can catch glimpses of the lovely River Dart.

In front of the collection of buildings with the clock tower, bear right towards Cornworthy and Dittisham. Cross the stream on a narrow stone bridge. At the next T-Junction, turn left to Cornworthy and Dittisham. At Cornworthy Cross, follow the road straight on to Dittisham and then turn right to East Cornworthy and Dittisham, passing the remains of an interesting-looking arched building. At Furzehill Cross, carry straight on towards East Cornworthy and Dittisham. At the next crossroads, go straight on to East Cornworthy and Dittisham. You are now descending, in modern terminology, a '15%' hill down towards the River Dart and the views are splendid. Wind down through the hamlet of East Cornworthy and over the little stone bridge. At Combe Cross, carry on to Dittisham and Dartmouth. At the next little junction, turn left signposted to Dittisham (**D**) arriving down by the River Dart where you could stroll along by the river.

At what looks like a fork, there is a small, obviously privately placed, sign pointing to the right-hand side to Dittisham on a stone wall and you should follow this direction. Just before getting to the church, turn right into Higher Street. Follow the signpost to Henborough and Dartmouth up the 1 in 5 hill. At the next crossroads, carry straight on — this is Bruckton Cross. Shortly afterwards, to the right, there is the Prehistoric Hill Settlement Museum signposted towards Capton. At the T-junction by the Sportsmans Arms public house, bear right at Henborough Post on the B3207. After just over a mile, at Alston Cross, turn left towards Blackawton, Strete, and Torcross. Shortly after, turn right signposted to Blackawton. At Trenchfurze Post Cross, continue on to Blackawton (**E**) passing the George Inn and the church..

Then, at Millcombe Corner, turn right towards Millcombe and East Allington. Descend the winding hill on the very narrow road. Go over the stone bridge and, at Millcombe Cross, go left and immediately right — that is, effectively straight on signposted to Abbotsleigh and Slapton. This is an awkward junction on a hill. Ignore the next right turn but, at Bow Cross, bear right signposted to Kingsbridge and East Allington. Carry straight on, signposted to Slapton and Kingsbridge, ignoring turnings to the left. At Wallaton Cross, turn left to Slapton and Torcross. When you reach Dittiscombe Cross, continue straight on towards Slapton and there are sea views in the distance ahead. At Higher Green Cross, carry straight on again towards Slapton through Lower Green Cross.

Carry on down the narrow road into Slapton village with its ruins standing on the hillside to the left and the church on the right. There is little parking in the village. Carry on to the coast road and turn left, passing the reedbeds which form part of Slapton Ley Nature Reserve (**F**). There is a possible stroll from the car park on the coast to Slapton by a ¼-mile footpath. Follow the coast road to Dartmouth. Even this main road has some spectacular bends. Pass through Strete bearing right

on the Dartmouth A379 road. Go through Blackpool Sands and Stoke Fleming. This is very narrow and twisting for an A road, and 'Bay View' and 'Channel View' guest houses abound. Note the right turning to Dartmouth Castle.

At the T-junction with the Totnes/Kingsbridge road, turn right towards the town centre and Paignton via the ferries. Follow the signs for the lower ferry. At the roundabout turn right for the lower ferry (**G**). The extraordinary little car ferry is tugged and guided by a separate boat attached to the platform by ropes. At the slip road the other side of the estuary is the station for the Dartmouth Steam Valley Railway. This is Kingswear and **Walk 3** begins from here. Follow the B3205 towards Paignton. At the T-junction turn left, signposted to Paignton and Brixham ★. At the T-junction with the A379, turn right to Paignton and Torquay. And, almost immediately, go right again on to the B3205 to Brixham at Hillhead. Continue down through the narrow streets of Brixham where the parked cars make the driving tricky. Carry straight on at the traffic lights. To complete the tour turn left as directed towards Paignton and Torquay on the A3022 at the next set of traffic lights into New Road and follow the coast road back to Paignton and Torquay. Alternatively, you could delay a while here for a stroll around Brixham.

Scale 1:250 000 or ¼ INCH to 1 MILE

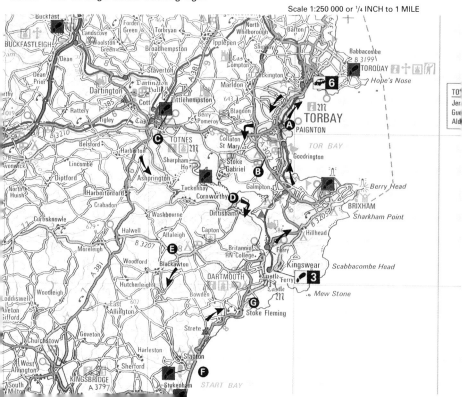

Tour 7
The Southern Tip

48 miles. Although the total mileage covered is not great, because of the nature of the roads, you should allow plenty of time for this tour. Alternatively, you could split it into two, beginning each 'half' at Kingsbridge. There are hairpin bends, narrow, twisting lanes, steep hills, and some of the junctions may cause you to make several manoeuvres to get round if you have a long car. In the high season, be prepared to follow queues of cars around the lanes, for some of the places on the way are very popular. And, of course, you should always be courteous to the local farm traffic which must use the roads. A bicycle may be the best way to complete this tour for the fitter travellers.

Leave Kingsbridge ★ on the A379 heading towards Torcross ★ and driving parallel to the river at first. Cross an arm of the Kingsbridge Estuary on an attractive stone bridge, pass through West and East Charleton, and go on through the village of Frogmore towards Dartmouth ★ and Stokenham ★ . Go through Chillington and Stokenham, ignoring the right-hand turning, and carrying on signposted to Dartmouth and Torcross at a mini-roundabout. The Church of St Michael and All Angels at Stokenham includes a possible stroll around the village.

At Torcross, make a short diversion by following the road around to the left. There is a small, limited-stay car park virtually opposite the Start Bay Inn, or a little further along the road there is a large public car park. There is a possible stroll along the lagoon side or along the beach and one should take in the memorial Sherman tank which was recovered from the sea locally, mainly through the efforts of a local landlord, Kenneth Small.

To return to the tour (**A**), drive back a little along the lagoon or, if you have not made the diversion, go straight on past Torcross post office and then turn right by the Village Inn up a steep, winding hill. At the T-junction of Mattiscombe Cross, turn left signposted to Start Point, East Prawle, East Portlemouth ★ , and Beesands. At the next crossroads, Beesonpool Cross, turn left to Beeson and Beesands. Turn left to Beesands at the next fork and then right towards Beesands and Beeson. Descend a steep and very twisting lane, and continue down the road to Beesands, turning right as you reach the coast. Having visited the coast, turn back into the village at the road from which you have just approached and turn left on the narrow road signposted 'Alternative Route to Kingsbridge'. At the next junction, turn right and, at the T-junction, turn left, turning left again at the next T-junction (Beesonpool Cross again) where there is a stop sign. Fork left, signposted to Start Point, Kellaton, and Hallsands. At Kellaton Cross continue round to the left , and at Bickerton Cross go straight on towards Hallsands South and Start Point. At Hollocombehead Cross, take the direction to Start Point. As you approach Start Point, the road surface deteriorates. At Start Point, there is a car park and a stroll to the lighthouse on tarmac, with a total distance there and back of about a mile; **Walk 4** also begins from here.

To continue on the tour, return back along the road from Start Point (**B**). At Hollocombehead Cross, once again, turn left signposted to Lannacombe. At Lannacombe Cross, turn sharp left back on yourself signposted to South Allington and Chivelstone. This is a quite remarkable, very narrow, tree-lined, overhung lane. At Southhall Cross, among farm buildings, turn left signposted to Chivelstone, East Prawle, and East Portlemouth. Having passed through South Allington, at the T-junction of Chivelstone Cross, turn left to East Prawle and East Portlemouth. At Knowle Fork continue on the way signposted to East Prawle. Just after the East Prawle village sign, turn left in front of a school house along an unsignposted road. Wind through the village on its very narrow roads and, at the next T-junction, turn right. Bear left at the next junction in front of a large thatched house. Turning left, there is car parking space by the village green, where there are also toilets, and there is a stroll of 1 mile to Prawle Point.

Returning from the car parking area (**C**), take the uppermost, left-hand road to the left of the post office and the Pigs Nose Inn (where you will get a warm welcome as well as good food and ale), bearing left with the Providence Inn on the right. At the next fork, which is signposted right to Kingsbridge, turn sharp left, and then at Vinnivers Cross, turn left towards West Prawle and East Portlemouth. Go straight on, passing the right turning to West Prawle. After a Z-bend, there is a sharp right-hand corner where the road narrows again. Continue on past the left turning to Gara Rock. At the next right-hand turning, Holset Cross, bear left and you soon arrive at the village of East Portlemouth. Drive on down into the village ignoring the turning to the left, and

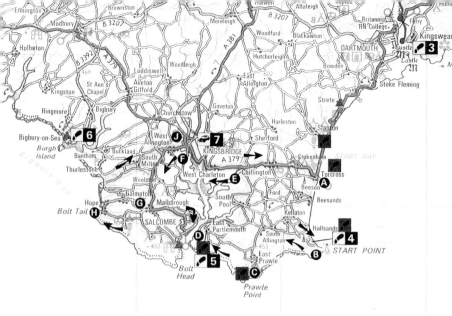

Scale 1:250 000 or ¼ INCH to 1 MILE

there are good views of Salcombe ★ .

Coming out of the village, follow the road round to the right and down the hill. At the left turning, signposted to the passenger ferry and Mill Bay (**D**), it is worth making a short detour. There is a very good little beach at Mill Bay where there is a National Trust car park and a stroll around the headland of Biddlehead Point to Sunny Cove and Blackstone. **Walk 5** also begins from here. Continue the tour from Mill Bay by driving back along the lane and turning left. The road continues to be narrow and twisting. Cross a small tidal ford, and then turn left signposted to Chivelstone and South Pool at Goodshelter Cross. At Devonshire Bridge Cross, go straight on towards South Pool. Descending the hill towards South Pool, the tower of the church rises up on the hill ahead. Bear left over the little bridge into South Pool village. Continue straight on at Long Cross and shortly after, straight on again at Leighlaneend Cross. Go over the little bridge and you are now back on the A379 where you turn left (**E**) to Kingsbridge.

Returning to Kingsbridge, take the A381 to Salcombe and Totnes ★ and, at the next mini-roundabout, carry straight on signposted to West Alvington and Salcombe on the A381 (**F**). Go through the village of West Alvington. In Malborough at Townsend Cross, bear left towards Salcombe (**G**), then left towards the town centre and the ferries, following the one-way system down through the town and back out again. Turn left at the fork towards North Sands, South Sands, and Bolt Head as well as towards Sharpitor. At the next T-junction, continue on to South Sands. Out of South Sands, take the very

sharp right-hand turn to Malborough. Pass the National Trust property of Tor Woods.

At Combe Cross, bear left to Rew and Malborough and, at Rew Cross, turn right towards Malborough. At Bolberry Cross turn left marked to Bolberry and Hope Cove ★ . Drive through the village of Bolberry and at the Bolberry village sign carry straight on towards Hope Cove, turning left towards Hope Cove and Galmpton. Pass the National Trust property of Hope Barton Farmland. You soon arrive at Hope Cove (**H**) and, on reaching the coast, turn right. At the next T-junction turn right signposted to Galmpton and Malborough. Continue through the village of Galmpton, bearing left towards Kingsbridge, Malborough, and Salcombe. Turn left at the next junction to South Huish and Thurlestone Sands. In South Huish, fork left down to the coast. At the T-junction, turn left and, at the next fork, turn right towards Thurlestone Sands. This is the National Trust Property of South Milton Sands which is pleasant for a stroll.

Drive along the rough track — avoiding forking left into the car park unless you intend to stop here — parallel with the coast to rejoin a tarmac lane the other side. At the T-junction in South Milton, turn left signposted to Churchstow at Thurlestone. Then turn right at Hillingsdown Cross to Churchstow. Go straight on at Upton Cross and, at Huxton Cross, turn right towards Kingsbridge and Salcombe. At the next T-junction turn right for Kingsbridge (**J**). At the next crossroads, Headiswell Cross, turn left for Kingsbridge. At the T-junction at West Alvington Butts, turn left back to Kingsbridge.

Tour 8
Okehampton and North Dartmoor

48 miles. This is a tour for confident drivers because some of the roads are very narrow and yet quite spectacular. Caravans are definitely out, and you are likely to meet farm traffic taking up the full width of the road. The farm workers do seem to make every effort to let cars pass, however. Allow plenty of time for there is much to stop and see. As usual, this trip is for fit cyclists only.

Start the tour from Okehampton ★ in the large, long-stay, pay-and-display car park in Market Street. Almost opposite the Market Street-West Street junction, there is the Tourist Information Office and Museum of Dartmoor Country Life. Turn left out of the car park and then left at the junction with West Street, following the old A30 road towards Exeter. Carry straight on across the new A30 bypass towards Sticklepath ★ . Shortly after the White House Transport Café, turn right (**A**) to Belstone ★ . Go over the cattle grid on to a narrow road with passing places and drive through a flat, gorse-clad, marshy area just before reaching a T-junction. If you turn right into the centre of Belstone, you could stroll around not least to look at the stone and wooden stocks.

To continue the tour, however, turn left towards Skaigh (pronounced skay) and

The barren landscape around Mary Tavy.

Sticklepath, along a very narrow, twisting, and descending lane through the beautiful wooded valley of the River Taw in Belstone Cleave. Emerging on to the old A30 again turn right in Sticklepath where you will find the Finch Foundry Museum. About ³/₄ mile beyond Ford Cross Garage, just over a small bridge, and on the apex of a left-hand bend, turn right to Throwleigh and Gidleigh ★ . This is an awkward turning and needs great care. Go over a little stone bridge and a cattle grid into typical Dartmoor in-country. At the next junction, signposted to the right, Gidleigh 2¹/₂ miles, continue straight on towards Throwleigh and Whiddon Down, and pass over another cattle grid. Throwleigh is another very attractive little thatched village with its church looking down on it. Emerging into the village, turn left down towards the stone cross and turn right on to a single-track lane, signposted to Providence, Wonson, Gidleigh, and Chagford ★ . At the next junction, continue straight on signposted to Gidleigh and Chagford. Pass the Northmoor Arms and turn left at the T-junction signposted to Chagford and Providence. The high moor can now be seen ahead and to the right.

Descend steeply on a twisting, narrow road into a lovely open vale. Go over a tiny bridge and, at the T-junction, turn left towards Chagford. Ignore any unsignposted lanes. Follow the road straight on to Chagford at the next junction. At the next crossroads, turn right towards Chagford and we can soon see the town nestling beneath the high moor. There is a 7-foot width restriction some way ahead at a bridge over the river. Descend towards Chagford, an interesting town visited on **Tour 2**. Shortly after the narrow bridge, you come to the next crossroads at which you go straight on (**B**), signposted to Princetown ★ . Continue to the right at the next T-junction where the left-hand route is signposted to Chagford and then carry straight on towards Fernworthy. At Tunnaford, either fork right to Fernworthy Reservoir ★ where there are pleasant strolls or longer walks to be enjoyed, or fork left to continue the tour.

Continue to follow the narrow, winding lane without diverting to right or left. There is the occasional reassuring signpost, suggesting that you are making for Princetown. Pass the imposing, large but sombre Lower Jurston Farm with its thatched farmhouse and stone-roofed outbuildings. Rise up the steep, winding hill from Jurston on to the high, windswept open moorland again. Eventually you emerge on to the B3212 (**C**) where you turn right signposted to Postbridge ★ and Princetown. Look out for the old stone crosses which mark the line of the Abbot's Way ★ as well as noticing the hut circles and stone circles which abound here. Pass the Warren House Inn, England's third highest pub, on the Postbridge road. There is a possible stroll down to some old tin workings by the stream from the Kings Oven car park before reaching the pub, and **Walk 8** also begins from here.

Pass the Widecombe ★ turn where **Tour 4** joins your route for a short distance as you approach Postbridge. Continue on the road signposted to Two Bridges and Princetown. At the T-junction with the B3357 turn right towards Princetown and, at the next turning, go left on to the B3212 signposted again to Princetown. The tower of the church can be seen but then suddenly to the right, there are the sombre and forbidding walls and buildings of Dartmoor Prison. Opposite the Devil's Elbow public house (**D**), there is a right turning on to the B3357 to Tavistock ★ past Dartmoor Prison Officer's Mess and the National Park information centre on the left. Be warned by the Police Notice: 'cars must not stop on this road'.

At the Rendelstones Cross T-junction with the B3212 and the B3357 turn left to Tavistock passing the car park from which **Walk 11** begins. Pass the disfiguring quarry

working of Merrivale near the Dartmoor Inn. Cross the cattle grid and, about ¹/₂ mile after entering the 30-mph restricted area, turn right on the A386 (**E**) to continue the tour back towards Okehampton or go straight on to visit Tavistock and stroll around the town. Turn right again at the next T-junction opposite the multistorey car park and pass the austere-looking Kelly college. Continue through Mary Tavy and look out for the chimney of Wheal Betsy ★ to the right.

Directly opposite the Dartmoor Inn, it is worth making a short diversion (**F**) left to Lydford ★. Pass the granite cross memorial. There is a car park on the left opposite the Three Castle Inn where you can stop to look at Lydford Castle.

Continue on A386 to Okehampton, passing the attractive thirteenth-century, stone and thatch Bearslake Inn. At Sourton Cross do not turn right on to the A30 to Okehampton but continue straight on the A386 signposted to Bideford. The open wound of Meldon Granite Quarry can be seen on the hills to the right. Turn right at the T-junction on A386 towards Hatherley, Torrington, and Bideford. Where the road forks for the A386 to Hatherley, continue straight on to Okehampton. Do not turn left on the A386. At the angled T-junction, rejoin the A30 back to Okehampton.

Scale 1:250 000 or ¹/₄ INCH to 1 MILE

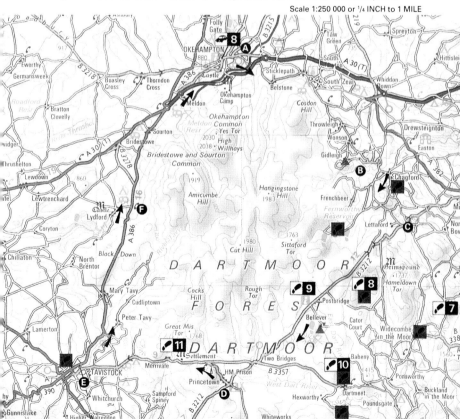

Tour 9
East of Plymouth

44 miles. This tour is hardly shorter in miles than most of the others in the book and, although you will encounter some very narrow lanes, you need allow less time for the trip because you return on the A38 trunk road. You will have the chance to explore the two picturesque villages on either side of the River Yealm, and you get a good impression of this corner of the South Hams as well as views across Plymouth Sound. Cyclists may wish to avoid the return trip on the busy A38.

Leave Plymouth ★ on the A379 heading towards Kingsbridge ★ and Plymstock. Cross an arm of Plymouth Sound, and turn immediately right at the next roundabout. At the traffic lights, turn right into Dean Park Road (**A**). At the next set of lights, bear right to Radford Park Road. Follow the road round to the right and continue down the Hooe Road, turning left just by the Fort Standford Leisure Centre. As you pass what must once have been a nineteenth-century fortress, Plymouth Sound can be seen to the right and Drake's Island is evident. The road winds upwards and is just wide enough for two cars to pass.

Bear right at Staddon Heights between the fortress and the golf course. Continue straight on through downland-like countryside and turn right at the T-junction towards Fort Bovisand. Turn left towards Wembury Beach and Langdon past the Old Tithe Barn which is now a bed and breakfast establishment. Follow the steep road down into Wembury ★ and Wembury Beach which is a National Trust property.

Turn up the hill past the Bay Cottage private hotel. Follow the road until you reach a T-junction taking the right of way left, signposted to Plymstock in Wembury Square (**B**). At the next T-junction in Plymstock, turn right towards Elburton, and you soon come to a roundabout with the A379 road at which you turn right towards Kingsbridge (**C**), and go into the South Hams district. Pass through Brixton and then turn right signposted to Newton Ferrers ★ on the alternative route for light vehicles (**D**). The road becomes very narrow especially over a little bridge. This road links with the B road from Yealmpton. Turn right towards Newton Ferrers and Noss Mayo and continue following the signs. Carry on down into the village of Newton Ferrers by bearing left where the 'No Through Road' sign occurs. There is very restricted and limited parking in the quayside area but it is a pleasant riverside

Scale 1:250 000 or ¼ INCH to 1 MILE

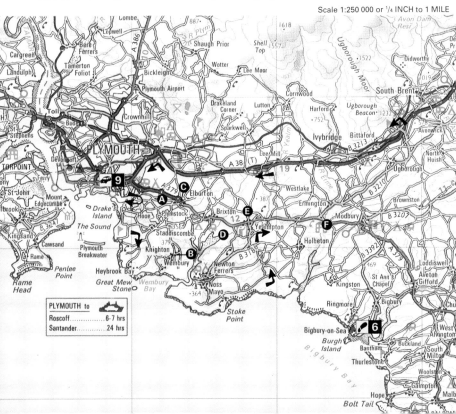

Views across Plymouth Sound towards Drake's Island can be had towards the beginning of the Tour.

village to stroll around.

From Newton Ferrers, drive back up the road until you reach the sign pointing right to Noss Mayo. Noss Mayo is on the other side of the River Yealm and both villages have their large churches. The road down into Noss Mayo is also narrow. Having crossed the Yealm, turn right to Noss Mayo on to the Stoke Road. Pass the church on the right, and continue on Stoke Road, branching left at the signpost to Noss Mayo. Bear left to Stoke and Holbeton at the Old Rectory signpost. At Stoke Cross, either continue on down to Stoke beach or turn left towards Mothercombe and Holbeton to return on the tour. There is a visitor's car park just before the final descent to Stoke beach and there is a stroll down to the little grey sandy beach by the caravan sight. It is a steep climb back up to the car park, however.

Rejoining the tour, take the fourth turning on the left at Alston Cross — the second and third turnings being very minor tracks. This road can be muddy and slippery from farm traffic and is very narrow and winding once again. Pass Alston Hall and, at the crossroads at the bottom of the valley, your road goes straight across. Do not be tempted to follow the road to the left. You are now following a winding, single-track road uphill between high hedges, and the surface is very poor.

Where a road comes in from the left, bear rightish to go straight on. Ignore the next right and left junctions. At the T-junction, turn left signposted to Yealmpton, Kingsbridge, and Plymouth. You soon join the A379 where you turn right (**E**).

At Modbury Cross (**F**), turn left on to the B3210 signposted to Totnes ★ and continue on towards Ugborough. Pass Ermington over the river bridge and you will then see the tall tower of Ugborough Church. The tour continues past Ugborough where there are fine old farm buildings on the left-hand side of the road at the bottom of the hill from Ugborough. At Bittaford Cross, turn left towards the A38 Exeter road following also the 'Leisure Drive' signs. At the T-junction at Wrangaton, turn left to Bittaford and Ivybridge on the B3213. Go under the railway bridge into Bittaford where the road runs parallel with the railway viaduct. Pass by the modern factory of Western Machinery which appears as though it might have been built around the chimney of a mining engine house. Continue on into Ivybridge ★ and follow the A38 and 'Leisure Drive' signs across the mini-roundabout towards Plymouth. At the main roundabout at the other side of the town, you pick up the A38 which takes you back to Plymouth.

Tour 10
Between the Tamar and Dartmoor

44 miles. Avoid starting or finishing this tour during the morning or evening rush-hour periods. You should make sure that your petrol tank is well filled before you embark on the moorland stretch of the tour beyond Horrabridge where, in places, the roads are so rough and narrow that there is barely enough tarmac for the wheels of one car. But the countryside is spectacular and there is a real sense of adventure in making that part of the trip. Here and there, too, it would be easy to dent a car on rocks jutting out from the sides of the lanes.

Leave Plymouth ★ heading north on the A386 towards Tavistock ★ , and past Plymouth Airport. After the Bellever roundabout, the countryside becomes more attractively Devonian and you soon enter the Dartmoor National Park ★ with the gorse-, heather-, and bracken-covered moorland to right and left where Dartmoor ponies graze peacefully alongside the busy main road. A little under a mile before reaching Yelverton at Roborough Rock, where there is a column dated 1837-97 VR, turn left (A) towards Crapstone and Buckland Monachorum ★ . It is possible here to stroll around on the open gorseland to explore the rock.

Go over a cattle grid and carry straight on round the bend where there is a junction to the left, but you bear right to Crapstone and Buckland Monachorum. Continue past the stone memorial cross and onwards to Crapstone and Buckland Monachorum. Entering the village of Crapstone, you can either bear right towards Buckland Monachorum or make a short diversion left to look at the National Trust property of Buckland Abbey ★ . Pass the gates of Crapstone House on the left and, at the next T-junction, divert right into Buckland Monachorum which is worth a stroll from the car park primarily intended for the use of church worshippers.

Return to the tour by driving back up the hill out of the village and then turn right. Very soon, turn left on to a single-track lane signposted to Milton Combe, Bere Alston ★ , and Plymouth. At the next T-junction in about 200 yards, turn right signposted to Bere Alston and descend into an attractive valley where the road narrows and twists, and is overhung by trees leaning out from the high banks.

After entering some woodland, turn left over the lovely Denham Bridge as signposted to Bere Alston ★ and Bere Ferrers ★ . There is now a steep 1 in 4 climb up out of the valley the other side. At the T-junction of Tavistock Cross, continue on into Bere Alston (B). Carry straight on at the next crossroads and down into the main part of the village.

Turn left into Fore Street, continuing out of the village up the hill. Take the next right turn to Weir Quay. Bear left at the T-junction, left at the next junction signposted to Weir Quay, and go downhill on a steep, narrow lane. On reaching the river, turn right and then follow the signposts once more back to Bere Alston. Weir Quay on the River Tamar is a pleasure boating area and is well worth a visit and a stroll. As you approach the village sign of Bere Alston, at a fork, go right signposted to Tavistock. Go straight across at the crossroads signposted to Tavistock. At the next junction follow the road down to the left indicated to Tavistock again. Then turn immediately right at the crossroads signposted to Tavistock. The road is signposted Gulworthy and Tavistock.

Continue following the main road signposted to Morwellham and Tavistock. Pass the Morwellham turn to the left and carry on towards Tavistock. Turn right at the cross roads towards Tavistock. Do not be tempted to go straight on towards Milton Abbot and Cornwall. At the give way and T-junction, turn right on to the A390 (C). Just past the tall church tower, turn right on to the A386 signposted town centre, Okehampton ★ , and Plymouth. Turn right at the little roundabout surrounding the statue of Sir Francis Drake and go over the canal bridge. Continue through Grenofen and enter the Dartmoor National Park. Cross Bedford Bridge over the River Walkham, and pass Magpie Leisure Park.

At Horrabridge, before reaching Yelverton, turn left signposted to Horrabridge (D). Follow the road downhill and over the little bridge bearing right, signposted to Sampford Spiney, Princetown ★ , and Tavistock. A little way up the hill by the sign for Jordan Lane, turn right towards Sampford Spiney and into the Bedford Road. At the first crossroads, continue straight on signposted to Tavistock. Go over the cattle grid and past the cross heading towards Sampford Spiney. At the next fork, by a triangle of grass and a group of trees behind, bear right towards Ward Bridge. Descending the hill, go over another cattle grid, following the road round to the left past the private drive of Wood Town, on a very narrow, steep, and twisting lane. Go over a bridge. At the

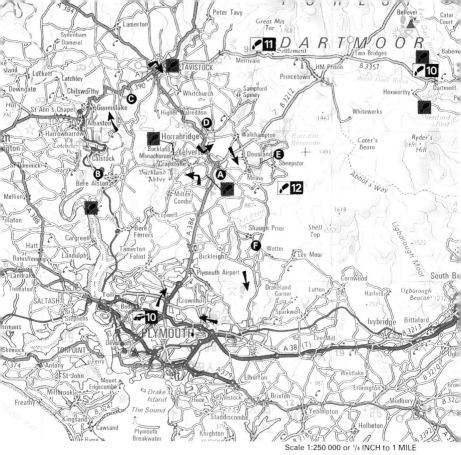

Scale 1:250 000 or ¼ INCH to 1 MILE

next crossroads, Crip Tor Cross, turn an awkward right signposted to Walkhampton. Drive over a little stream where, off to the left, there is a clapper bridge.

Fork left at the next junction up the hill through gate posts and across two cattle grids. As you descend towards the village of Walkhampton, you can see the church tower ahead. Turn left and then left again by the stone cross signposted to Princetown and Dousland. At the actual crossroads with the B3212 carry straight on signposted to Burrator ★ and Sheepstor passing the Burrator Inn. Go across another crossroads and you come to another fork where you go left, signposted to Burrator and Sheepstor. Cross the cattle grid. Turn right to cross the impressive Burrator Dam (E) — built between 1923 and 1928 — towards Sheepstor. **Walk 12** overlooks this area and the reservoir.

Continue round to the right at the next fork, past the church and the stone cross, and then ignore the right turning, carrying straight on along the line of a little stream. At the next fork go right. Head towards Cadover and Ivybridge ★ by a right fork. At the staggered crossroads, turn left towards Cadover and Ivybridge. Turn left at the next T-junction signposted to

Cadover Bridge, Lee Moor, and Cornwood ★. Go over Cadover bridge and bear right, or stop for a riverside stroll here. Pass another stone cross, and you can see Plymouth Harbour straight ahead. Where the next right turning appears, carry straight on towards Shaugh Prior. Turn right at the T-junction to Shaugh Prior at Beatland Cross. Continue down into the village (F) and, shortly after the derestricted sign, the road bears right down the hill and then right again.

Cross the stone bridge and follow the road round to the left. Ignore two right forks and the last left fork. Carry on over a block bridge and turn left away from the village of Bickleigh. Descend a very narrow lane and, at the T-junction, turn right. Go over a stone bridge with a 7-foot width restriction and continue up another steep narrow lane. Emerging on to a more substantial minor road, turn right. After some distance, go down Borringdon Hill to another T-junction and turn right to Colbrook. Turn left at the next T-junction and cross the railway, turning right at the next T-junction towards Plymouth. Then, immediately after, go right (G) at the mini-roundabout to pick up the dual carriageway which leads back to Plymouth.

103

Walking in South Devon and Dartmoor

It is well known that the climate of the south-west peninsula is generally mild and moist. Remember, though, that Dartmoor rises to heights of over 2000 feet (600 m) and, at High Willhays, reaches 2039 feet (619 m). Consequently, although the weather, even at its worst, is wet and windy rather than bitterly cold as it is in the more northerly upland regions of Britain, the effects of wind chill can dramatically reduce body temperature to dangerously low levels very quickly. Treat Dartmoor with respect! Unless you are proficient in the use of map and compass, do not venture on to the moors in misty conditions or when the visibility is poor for any reason. Because, in many parts of the moor, there are few obvious landmarks to help you navigate, it is all too easy to lose your bearings and, even though you may only be a mile or two from a road, that is no guarantee of safety. Dartmoor sheep and ponies spend their lives on the moor and they are accustomed to its more treacherous side but, as any Dartmoor farmer will tell you, they still lose stock through injury or exposure.

There is one Dartmoor hazard which is made much of but which, apart from in deep snow, is easy enough to avoid — the ironically named 'feather bed'. The feather bed is a water-filled hollow in the granite which may reach depths of several metres — well over the height of a man and deep enough to drown a horse. But pools, however deep should not be a problem unless, like feather beds, they do not look like pools. The surface of a feather bed is a thick mat of sphagnum moss which, to the unwary, looks as solid as the surrounding moorland. There is a difference between a feather bed and the greenish-brown, heather-clad moorland — it is bright green! When covered with snow, however, a feather bed can not be distinguished from any other part and at least one experienced local moorland walker has found its icy cold water above his head; and it gets worse, once a person or an animal has broken through the sphagnum mat, it tends to close again. In the case of this walker, he was only saved by catching his foot on a rock as he fell down so that he was able to clamber out again, freezing cold but alive.

Walking along South Devon's coastal paths is a pleasure not to be missed by anyone but the sufferer from vertigo. Essentially, walking a cliff path should be safe enough but take care; it is all too easy to miss one's footing on the edge or to be so captivated with a soaring fulmar that a break in the path is overlooked. Nor should you underestimate the arduousness of walking in Devon; it may not be a county of lofty mountains but the long, steep ups and downs of Devon's rolling hills can drain the strength even from a seasoned walker's legs. And, although in this guide, the walks have been designed to give the average family walker a pleasant ramble

A group of walkers stop at the 'letterbox' at Cranmere Pool.

lasting no more than, say, half a day, **Walk 6** is long and quite demanding. Never attempt a walk which is longer or tougher than that which the weakest member of your party can comfortably achieve — even if you are not actually putting yourself or others at risk, it simply isn't any fun to be walking with aching limbs, blistered or wet feet, or having to listen to the complaints of someone else who is tired and miserable!

What you will need

In almost every town now, outdoor shops appear packed to the gunwales with a bewildering array of brightly coloured, expensive, hi-tec equipment. You should not need to spend a great deal of time or money assembling the equipment for the walks in this book but there is a small number of items which will make your walk more comfortable, safer, and above all more enjoyable.

The most important item to get right is footwear. For these walks, a good pair of lightweight walking shoes or boots is best. Either read some equipment reviews in outdoor magazines or go to a reputable outdoor centre and ask for advice. Essentially, you have two sets of choices to make: boots or shoes? leather or reinforced fabric? Shoes and reinforced fabric are lighter and need little or no breaking in but shoes do not provide ankle support and the fabric boots are not really waterproof unless they have a (expensive) Goretex lining. Leather boots are heavier; they do need breaking in; but they provide better protection for the feet, they are more waterproof, and with care, a good pair will last you many years and many miles. In every case, you should look for a sole, such as Vibram or Klets, which gives good grip and does not clog. Under your boots, you could wear just a single pair of

The vast, empty area around Hound Tor is typical of the majestic scenery of Dartmoor. But do keep note of your path, as it is easy to lose your sense of direction.

loop-stitch, wool-mix socks although some people prefer a second pair of thin socks beneath.

Do not wear denim jeans for walking; the stiff material can chafe but, more importantly, wet jeans are very cold and uncomfortable. There is a wide variety of reasonably priced poly-cotton walking trousers available now or you may prefer the traditional 'moleskin' or woollen variety. A comfortable wool, cotton, or poly-cotton shirt with some kind of fibre-pile, fleece, or woollen sweater should be all you need for your upper body but, if you perspire heavily, then a non-absorbant vest which wicks the moisture away from your skin is a good idea. And take a light-weight waterproof (including overtrousers for a long walk); not only will it keep you dry but it will prevent wind chill if the temperature should fall. PU or neoprene-coated nylon are the cheapest but one of the breathable fabrics, such as Goretex, is more comfortable if you are likely to perspire.

It's a good idea to take map and compass, as well as this guide, but only if you know how to use them properly — the guide should be enough to enable you to navigate the walk. Spare food, a small first-aid kit, perhaps a torch or emergency whistle, and a hat should complete the kit — sun hat for the summer and balaclava for the winter.

Finally, you'll need a rucksack to carry everything in; a rucksack is more comfortable than any other kind of bag and leaves your hands free. Again seek advice, buy the best and most comfortable that you can afford but, above all, do not buy a sack which is too big for your needs — you'll be tempted to fill it.

Walk 1
Beer Head and South Down Common

Although this is a short walk, because of the steep ascents and descents on and from the cliff top, it is surprisingly demanding and should not be attempted lightly. You will need to cross several stiles on the coast path. Starting from the attractive little fishing and holiday village of Beer, the walk includes some of the best of the East Devon coastal scenery with fine views westwards to Branscombe Mouth and beyond, and eastwards past Seaton and the coast of Dorset. In good weather allow 1½-2 hours and a little more if there is any sea mist.

Beer ★ (192) (SY 2389) is on **Tour** 1. It can be reached using the B3174 road leading from the main A3052 road between Sidmouth ★ and Seaton ★, or along the coast road about 1 mile west of the larger holiday resort of Seaton. Park in the so-called Cliff-Top car park at Beer (**A**) and look for the wooden signpost indicating 'Coast Path Branscombe Mouth 1²/₃ miles'. Go down three or four concrete steps to join the path. Turn right and, just before a large permanent caravan site, turn left as the coast path sign suggests. Follow the well-marked coast path. Go through a wooden kissing gate and the track enters a grassy meadow. Looking to the left, you can see the holiday and urban development of Seaton, whereas Beer harbour is tucked away in the cove nearby. Continue following the track where acorns and yellow waymarks appear on stiles and gates. As you continue on there are fine coastal views back across Seaton and beyond. Walk on through the gorse-cloaked, grassy way on the high raised beach. As you approach the area below the coast guard lookout post (**B**), there are fine views across Branscombe Mouth and beyond. The cliff here has fallen, leaving behind its stacks and undercliff not dissimilar to the famous undercliff at Lyme Regis, although the rock here is chalk with its dotted lines of flints.

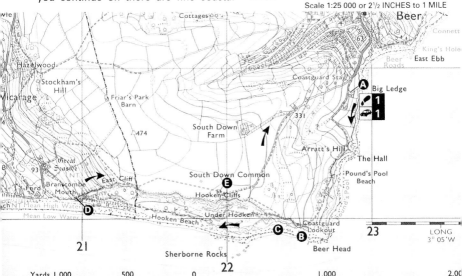

Scale 1:25 000 or 2½ INCHES to 1 MILE

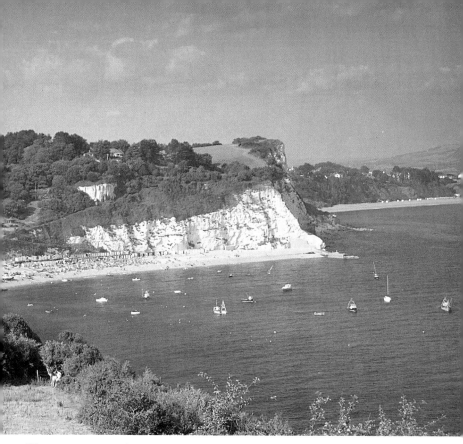

When you come to a three-way wooden signpost (**C**), with Hooken Cliffs straight on up the hill, the coast path to Branscombe Mouth takes you left across a stile. It seems hardly worth it on such a short walk, but it would be possible here to take a short cut by following the path up to Hooken Cliffs and turning right at the top. The path now descends steeply on a narrow track down past the back of the stacks towards Branscombe Mouth. Carry on down on a winding way into a woody combe via some cliff steps. The white chalk cliffs rise mightily to the right and there seems to be a cave ahead. Follow the path as it winds its way down and then runs parallel to the stony beach below. This is Hooken Beach. At the wooden signpost just before reaching Branscombe Mouth, carry straight on following the coast path towards the Mouth itself through a track by some permanent caravans. Going on down towards the Mouth on a partially concreted lane, you will pass a number of beach huts and caravans. The track soon becomes fully concreted. At a four-way signpost by a cattle grid (**D**), turn back on yourself up a very steep hill towards the top of the cliff. It is signposted to Hooken Cliffs and Beer. Pass through a hunting gate and aim up the grassy slope

Looking back towards the beach at Beer from the coast path.

to some steps. Go over a stile and climb the rest of the steps. The steps eventually come to an end and, approaching the top of the grassy slope, bear half right. Follow the broad grassy track along the cliff top aiming towards a wooden gate ahead.

Follow the indistinct path across the grassy meadow, keeping the cliff-edge fence about 10 yards to your right. Aim towards the coast guard lookout buildings. To the right of the buildings you can see a wooden signpost on the cliff edge ahead. From the cliff top here there are fine views back along the coast and the sea air is invigorating up here. When you reach the signpost by the coast guard lookout buildings (**E**), take the direction indicated half left 'Public Footpath' rather than the direction signposted to Beer. You are now veering away from the coast. Aim towards a farm track leading to a gate. Go across a cattle grid or through the gate and follow the farm lane. From here there are good views down over Seaton. This is South Down Common. Pass by the driveway to South Down Farm on the left and bear right down the road to the Cliff-Top car park.

Walk 2
Harcombe Woods and Valleys

With such superb walking to be found along South Devon's often spectacular coast, as well as the irresistible draw of Dartmoor's lonely heights, it is tempting to look no further for good walking in this part of the county. Here, however, is an inland walk far from the moor, which takes the walker up and down a lovely valley with woods which, in early summer, are heady with the scent of bluebells. After wet weather, parts of this walk can be very muddy, and between Lower Swetcombe Farm and Harcombe, the route can be a little tricky to follow. Allow 3 hours.

The little village of **Harcombe** (192) (SY 1590) is just to the north of the A3052 which forms the southern arm of Tour **1**. About ¼ mile east of where the A3052 crosses the River Sid just by Steven's Cross Garage, turn left and then take the next right into Harcombe. The walk begins near the Snod Brook by Harecombe Farm (**A**). There is no car park here but there is room for one car by the bridge.

Walk up the private road to Paccombe House Farm. All around is pleasant farmland and woodland. Where the drive goes straight on across a cattle grid to Paccombe House Farm itself, fork left following the public bridleway uphill and over another cattle grid. You will then find yourself on an ascending gravel lane. Pass through a gate just before reaching a house, and turn right following the bridle path and footpath sign, keeping the house on the left. Pass through another gate and bear left at the fork, again following the sign. Where a lane goes down to the right, go straight on uphill. Pass by fields which may be populated by donkeys. There is lovely bluebell woodland here as you walk along the north bank of the most attractive valley of the Snod Brook. Nearing the top of the lane, pass through another gate.

Emerging on to a minor road (**B**), turn left and walk down the road for about 100 yards, when you turn right following the public footpath sign which leads to the

Scale 1:25 000 or 2½ INCHES to 1 MILE

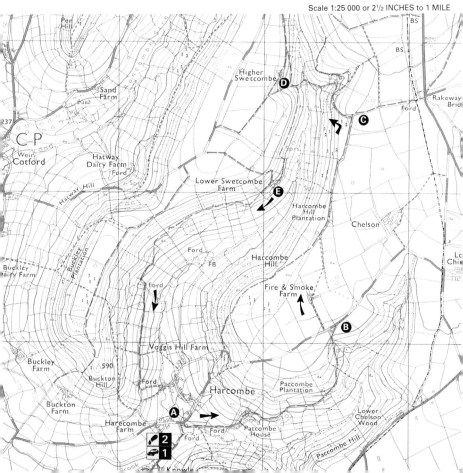

The lush greens of the foliage, lit by shafts of sunshine, at Harcombe Hill.

intriguingly named Fire and Smoke Farm. Follow the farm lane around the left-hand side of the farm house. Go through a gate at the back of the house and aim diagonally across the field to the far corner where there is some woodland on the left and a line of trees and a hedge meeting it from the right.

Cross the stile in the corner of the field joining a broad bridle track in a narrow band of woodland forming part of Harcombe Hill plantation. Turn right. This is a pleasant track through the woods although, because of the churning of horses' hoofs, it is very sticky after rain. Go through a gate continuing straight along the woodland track. Where this stretch of woodland comes to an end and you arrive at a T-junction in the tracks, before a bank and an open field beyond (**C**), take the left-hand track. Again, this is a muddy bridleway. The track veers right and descends the hill. To the left there are wonderful woods reaching down to the river. Where the track makes an obvious fork, take the left-hand, lower fork heading downhill. On reaching a gate, go through it and turn left as indicated by the yellow arrows just before some seemingly derelict buildings, and continue following the broad bridle track and yellow waymarks downhill.

On reaching a stream towards the bottom of the valley, veer left between two wooden posts and cross the stream. Follow the track uphill as it quickly broadens out into a wider bridleway. A short distance up the hill, a track joins from the left (**D**) and you should take it heading back along the river valley. It is a bramble- and conifer-lined track which could become overgrown when the shrubbery is at its height. Carry on more or less southwards down the side of the river valley. The path continues through most delightful woodland where the resinous smell of conifers adds to a walker's enjoyment. Emerging from the woodland, go through a gate and walk along the obvious path with meadowland to the right and a little woodland down the valley to the left. You will soon arrive at the buildings of Lower Swetcombe Farm (**E**).

Just before reaching the house, cross the concrete farm road and go up the hill on the grassy track ahead taking you behind the buildings themselves. Go through the gate at the back of the buildings and aim for the next gate where a square yellow waymark can be seen on the gatepost. Continue on down the lane towards the woodland following the contours of the hill. Do not go through the gate with the yellow arrow. The arrow actually points to the right where the path can be seen at the edge of the wood, but it is completely overgrown at this point. Ignore the path and bear to the right keeping the wood close on the left-hand side. This part of the route is roughish pasture on a slope and easy walking. Keep the wood to the left until you see another waymarked gate. Go through the gate and, still with the wood on the left, cross a stile, and then bear left into the wood where there is a small latched gate. Go through this gate and then bear right out of the wood to another gate. After passing through this one, turn sharp left downhill to pick up the path that runs through a row of trees. At the bottom of this short path, turn downhill and cross a ford at the bottom of the hill. At this point the well-defined track to Harcombe can be seen.

Walk 3
Dartmouth Estuary, the Coast, and Higher Brownstone

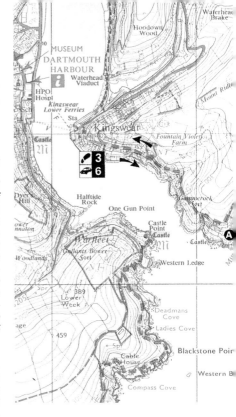

This walk includes one of the finest stretches of South Devon's Coast Path. With woodlands and cliffs, masses of wild flowers, and the accompanying calls of gulls and other seabirds, it is well worth taking plenty of time to enjoy it. Although the geography of the coast forces you to take a zig-zagging, upping and downing route which can be very demanding, the scenery all around more than compensates for the effort involved. Just at the end of the walk, there is a descent on a narrow footpath where the ground is littered with smooth boulders which are very slippery in wet weather. Allow 4-5 hours.

Kingswear (202) (SX 8850) is on **Tour 6**. Park in either of the pay car parks in Kingswear just before reaching the ferry terminal and the Dart Valley Steam Railway ★ Station. By Kingswear Hall, the Ship Inn, and the church look for Church Lane which is signposted 'Coast Path'. Shortly, where the lanes pass either side of an oblong stone house, fork right into Beacon Road as signposted and continue along the narrow lane which then becomes a walkway. Emerging on to another narrow lane, turn right following the yellow-arrowed and acorn-marked posts. Follow the lane past Brookhill Flats and up the hill. Through the trees there are now views of Dartmouth ★ Castle across the Dart.

Where the houses thin out, and you come to a deepish little valley at Warren Woods (**A**), turn right along the coast path signposted to Froward Point, going down some wooden steps into the ravine. By a cattle grid across a lane, continue down the steps ahead. On reaching the bottom of the valley, carry on to another partly metalled track towards the remains of a tiny castle-like building. Then, just before a gate, turn left as signposted and go up some steep steps. At the top of the steps continue following the path uphill into some woodland. This attractive mixed woodland is a nature reserve managed by the Devon Wildlife Trust. Continue to follow the acorn posts as you undulate and wind through the wood. From here there are good views across the mouth of the estuary towards Blackstone Point and Combe Point. Notice the fine stands of old

Scots Pines. The heady scent of the sea and pine resin adds to your enjoyment.

Go over the V-shaped stile into the National Trust property of Higher Brownstone. At a fork in the path, a waymark post leads you downhill on the right fork and the walking becomes ever-more enjoyable. The woodland is carpeted with wild flowers. You soon come to the complex of block houses and gunnery emplacements left over from World War 2 of Inner Froward Point (**B**). At the four-way signpost, take the right-hand route signposted 'Coast Path to Brixham 8¾ miles', and just beside some of the blockhouses, turn right down some steps towards the sea. The way takes you down a sometimes slippery ramp with its railway-like tracks. As the rocks of Mew Stone come into view, almost along the line of some railings, watch out for the wooden way post taking you left up a fork. At another waymark post by a fork, take the lower, right-hand track as indicated. The colours are quite wonderful with the bright-yellow gorse, punctuated by the deep blue haze of the bluebells, white campion, and more. In summer, there are the tall yellow spikes of the dark mullein to compensate for the loss of the spring flowers.

The coast path signs now point you towards Pudcombe Cove (**C**) with its rock arch below. Go over a stile and into some

Scale 1:25 000 or 2½ INCHES to 1 MILE

woodland following the track downhill. At the shoreward end of Pudcombe Cove, continue on a tarmacked path. Just before reaching some gates, the coast path bears to the right, waymarked by acorn signs. If you have no dog with you and you are either a member of the National Trust or are willing to pay the entrance fee, it is possible here to make a short cut back to your starting point and, at the same time, pay a visit to Coleton Fishacre Garden ★. This is open on Wednesdays, Fridays, and Sundays between 11.00 am and 6.00 pm from 1 April to 31 October.

Carrying on with the walk, go through the V-shaped stile, and you can see the small double crags out to sea of Eastern Black Rock. Heading uphill once again, you emerge on to open, rolling grassland sloping down to the sea. At Ivy Cove, there is a three-way wooden footpath sign pointing on to Scabbacombe Sands 1¼ miles on the coast path. Walk on past the impressive scar of Ivy Cove. By a little cove, where there is a drainage outlet pipe, the direction could be confused. In fact, you head up the cliff ahead towards a stile. Go over the stile and pull up the steep, winding track above the cliff. At a wooden footpath sign indicating Scabbacombe Sands to the right and Coleton Camp car park straight ahead, go straight on along the top of the cliff. Nearing the top of the

hill you will come to another three-way post, pointing straight on to Scabbacombe Sands and left to Coleton Camp car park (**D**); turn left across the stile and up over the field. Follow the grassy track uphill with the field boundary and hedge on your immediate right. Go through the gate where there is also a high ladder stile. Continue straight on but look to your left horizon and you will see a conical tower.

Go through another gate or over the stile and walk on up the lane and through Coleton Camp car park. At the crossroads with a minor road, walk straight on following the Higher Brownstone car park sign passing the other side of the National Trust property Coleton Fishacre Garden.

Follow the Private Road, which is a public footpath, down towards Higher Brownstone Farm. Continue following the public footpath towards Kingswear. At Lower Brownstone Farm, bear rightish in front of the farm house by a stone wall and follow the public footpath direction. Go on down the lane which is gravelly at first and then concreted. By a house, dive into the narrow footpath between hedges. Go over a little bridge by a white house and you join the tarmac lane which we left at the beginning of the walk to descend down into the valley. Go on up the lane and below in the valley you can see the little castle which you passed by earlier.

111

Walk 4

Start Point and Lannacombe Bay

Devon is a hilly county so much of the walking is quite arduous, but the superb coastal walking is reward enough if you have a reasonable head for heights. Although the cliff path is perfectly safe, it is as well to take care crossing some of the slippery schists. If you do not wish to have a return which involves some road walking, you could do worse than simply to retrace your steps along the coast path from Lannacombe Bay and enjoy a different perspective of the same section of path. In places at Woodcombe, the going is wet and rocky so it could be slippery. Allow 3-4 hours for the complete walk.

Start Point ★ (202) (SX 8337) is on **Tour 7**. Begin the walk from the pay car park at Start Point and walk down the road towards the lighthouse. This is signposted 'Coastpath to Lannacombe'. As you continue to walk down the path, the lighthouse is concealed behind the rocks and, just past a wooden hut, fork right on to the coast path (**A**). Simply follow the yellow arrows and acorn waymarks. This now is coast walking at its best along a narrow path below the top of the cliff. Look on to the rocks below for the roosting gulls, cormorants, and shags, and in spring stunted bluebells and primroses line the cliff. Presumably, this must once have been wooded if bluebells grow here and those that survive have adapted to resist the salt spray and winds. Reassuring acorn posts continue to mark the way and there are dramatic gullies down to the sea below. After ½ a mile or so of level walking the path begins slowly to descend towards a grassy plateau some 20-30 feet above the sea.

Gannets soar and wheel above the sea in search of their fish prey in the water below. Passing around Pear Tree Point, Great Mattiscombe Sand can be seen ahead. Stay on the path above the beach. Here there is a possible shortcut back to the car park. The lower route continues along the coast path towards Lannacombe with the intriguing twin stacks, known as Two Stones, remaining as all that is left of the fallen cliffs. Go over the triangular wooden style through the wall at Two Stones and continue following the acorn posts. Pass by Limpet Cove with King's Head Rock towering above the gorse-clad slopes. The cottages at Lannacombe can now be seen clearly. Below the King's Rock the path becomes a grassy cart track. The cliff continues past the shelly, sandy beach known as Harris's Beach and the

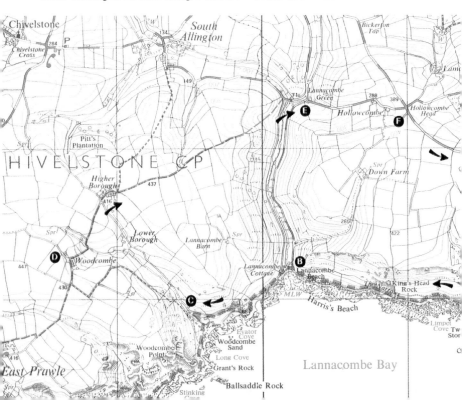

path descends gently to Lannacombe Bay. Follow the acorns down towards the beach and then follow the wooden signposts indicating 'Coastpath to Prawle Point ★ '. Carry on up the path past the cottage following the yellow arrows and acorns. This is the approach lane to the next house. Pass on the seaward side of the house following more acorn-marked posts.

If you are continuing with the whole route, walk behind a bungalow and go on up the grassy lane. Cross the small stream and an acorn-marked stile (**B**). At the wooden signpost follow the Public Footpath to the right towards Woodcombe. We now leave the coast path on a narrow, shrub-, bluebell-, and primrose-lined path going steeply uphill (**C**). After the climb, the path levels out and the valley opens up to the right with the white buildings of Lower Borough to be seen ahead. Coming to a T-junction with a farm track where there is a gate on the right, turn left as the yellow arrows suggest on a tractor-rutted lane. Pass through a gate and continue onwards following the yellow arrows and ignoring the track to the left. By another gate into a field with some corrugated iron machinery sheds, follow the lane as it turns right. At the next T-junction in the lanes, follow the way signposted towards Lannacombe Green by turning right, and then walk into the midst of the farm buildings of Woodcombe (**D**). Just before reach-

Scale 1:25 000 or 2½ INCHES to 1 MILE

ing some green-painted metal storage silos, turn right across the cattle grid and turn right again following the blue waymarks this time so that you almost walk around three sides of the farm. Continue on down the concrete road and over the next cattle grid. As you approach the top of the hill, the concrete soon peters out to become a gravelly track. The lane takes you to the back of the collection of buildings comprising Higher Borough.

At the crossroads in the lanes continue straight on following the blue arrows towards the back of the farm buildings. Bear right along the lanes around the buildings and in front of the house and farmyard; take the right-hand of the two gates following the blue marker — it is not altogether obvious to which gate the arrow refers. Follow the track along the left-hand side of the field and you can now see the BBC twin masts which are close to your starting point. At the end of the field, carry straight on through a gate and into a hedge-lined lane signposted with the blue waymark. Emerging from the grassy lane, you come to a little clearing with two gates and a lane going off to the left. Go into the field with the left-hand gate as the blue arrows indicate. Follow the rutted track along the right-hand edge of the field with fine views across Devon countryside inland to the left. Pass through the gap in the next field boundary, continuing along the track with the bank and hedgerow on the right. Pass through the next farm gate and go on down the lane to another gate. Go through the gate and into the open field, following the track in the grass and keeping the fence on your left. In the corner of the field just before the land drops away steeply, turn left aiming down into the gully ahead. Descend steeply into the gully towards the little copse in the valley and some houses which can just be made out. Walk between two patches of gorse and then pick up a narrow, indistinct path down through the left-hand patch of gorse until you pick up the waymarks again as you approach the sound of the stream. Now the path contours along the valley side with the sound of the stream to the right. Emerge on to a narrow lane through a gate (**E**). Turn right on to a metalled lane descending towards the river. Cross the little stream on a pretty lane.

Shortly, you will come to Lannacombe Cross at which you turn right signposted to Start Point and Southhall Sands. Just follow the road back to the carpark, forking left where a signpost points right to Lannacombe. Nearing the top of the hill at Hollowcombe Head Cross (**F**), turn right to Start Point.

113

Walk 5

Portlemouth Down and a Lovely Green Lane

Mill Bay itself is an attractive place to begin a very pleasant round trip. This is a delightful walk in spring and early summer when the gorse is at its golden best and clouds of yellow cloak the sloping cliffs, and when the green lane towards the end of the walk is ribboned with a galaxy of wonderful wild flowers. There are one or two moderately steep climbs on the way but, generally, it is an easy walk on good paths. Allow about 2 hours unless you decide to extend the walk further along the coast path towards Pig's Nose and beyond.

Begin the walk in the National Trust car park at **Mill Bay** (202) (SX 7438) on **Tour 7** for which, during the season, there is a charge for non-members. Walk back towards the beach, and then follow the acorn-marked 'Coast Path' signpost towards Gara Rock. Do not take the next fork left pointing to the 'Upper Cliff Path' but continue on around to the right. The wooded cliffside path enjoys fine views over the estuary with Salcombe ★ on the far bank, a lovely blue-bell-hazed woodland on the left, and we can also look over the sands of Mill Bay. At the next fork, go left avoiding the track down to the beach at Sunny Cove (**A**). There are splendid views over Salcombe Harbour and some sandy beaches, as well as luxuriant palms which can grow in this 'English Riviera' climate. The path continues through pleasant bluebell woods above the cliffs. There are seats at which to stop, rest, and enjoy the views and the sea air. Look out into the harbour as you walk and you will see the line of rocks which constitute The Bar.

Passing The Bar, the countryside opens out and, although we are still walking above the shoreline, we are among gorse-, bramble-, and bracken-clad, sloping cliffs, and the good path makes for easy walking even though it is undulating. The rocks of Start Point can be seen clearly ahead in the far distance and, behind, the rocks of Bolt Head, Mew Stone, and Little Mew Stone are obvious enough. Here, as you walk along the slopes of Portlemouth Down, the land seems to reach out its fingers into the sea like a hand grasping

Scale 1:25 000 or 2½ INCHES to 1 MILE

the waves. On the Down just beyond the rocks on the shoreward side called the Bull, you come to an acorn post and waymark post where the high-level path joins your route from the left. Carry on towards Gara Rock. When you see the sands of Abraham's Hole, the path begins to rise uphill

and heads a little inland. Continue on, ignoring any paths joining from the left until you reach an acorn post pointing down towards the bay. There is a footpath sign pointing uphill (**B**) towards a little round, white-painted summerhouse with a pointed thatched roof. Follow the path uphill, including rising up some steps in the track. At the top of the steps in front of the Gara Rock Hotel, turn left at the wooden signpost towards Mill Bay. Very shortly, you will arrive in the hotel's car park at which you should turn right and continue on up the minor road for about 400 yards. After a right-hand bend in the road, you soon come to a wooden footpath marker which points left through a gate and across farmland (**C**).

Go across the field on the well-defined track to the next stile and gate. Go over the stile, bearing slightly to the right and follow another well-defined path through a meadow towards a clump of low trees and a gate. Go through the gate or over the stile and carry along the public footpath which follows the tree-lined track. Emerging from the next gate, fork left into the sunken lane where there is rolling sheep-grazing on the right as you descend towards Mill Bay again and the forest ahead. This is a truly lovely English lane in springtime with bluebells and primroses lining the banks on either side, and, to add to the colour, there is red campion and white stitchwort with the lovely pale-green fronds of the hart's-tongue fern emphasizing the luxuriance. Passing through a line of iron posts, you soon arrive back at the car park.

A view of the boat-filled Salcombe Harbour.

115

Walk 6
Bigbury-on-Sea to Erme Mouth

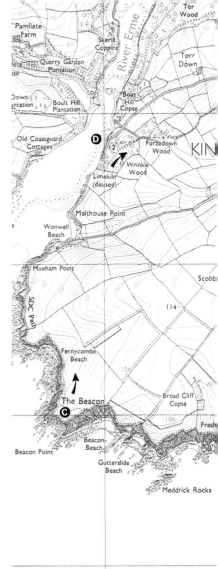

Scale 1:25 000 or 2¹/₂ INCHES to 1 MILE

This is a challenging walk which should only be attempted by the fit and able. Certainly, vertigo sufferers would do well to avoid this part of the coast path. It is, however, satisfying and most enjoyable with lovely coastal scenery, good inland walking, and a variety of geology and wildlife to add spice to the trek. It is even possible to emulate long-distance walkers here by wading across the Erme Mouth. Allow 4-5 hours.

There is some free parking at **Bigbury-on-Sea** ★ (202) (SX 6544), just before you reach the coast, or there is a large pay car park up the hill. Look for the coast path signposts pointing the way eastwards to Challaborough. Across the sand and the causeway is Burgh Island ★ with its Pilchard Inn and little castle on the top of the islet. Keeping the sea and the island at your left hand, follow the road or the shoreside track until you come to another wooden signpost pointing up the road 'Coast Path Challaborough'. Go into a 'no through road', again following the coast path signs. Go through a gate following the lane down to Challaborough. Continue on down the lane behind the beach following it round as it runs parallel with the coast. Just past the beach, turn left and then immediately right close to a building as indicated (**A**). Descend steeply down to Ayrmer Cove (**B**) and continue on the coast path behind the stony beach. There is a possible shortcut here by turning right on the footpath to Ringmore village.

Go over a little footbridge behind the beach, climbing up away from the beach again, and follow the coast path signposts to Wonwell. You will soon dive downhill again, this time behind Westcombe Beach, ready for the long haul up the other side to the top of Hoist Point. Go up the steep, plank-supported steps. Once more the path winds downhill into a valley and up yet again, and you will soon see Meddrick Rocks just offshore. You quickly reach the dizzy heights of Beacon Point (**C**) more than 300 feet above sea level. On the other side of the bay of the River Erme, the cliffs are lower and the beach of Erme Mouth can be seen. Follow the broad, grassy track which descends gently down to Wonwell Beach. You will pass through a small copse of stunted, lichen-draped blackthorn and there are fine views up the valley of the River Erme.

Go over the stile following the acorn waymarks along the coast path. Passing Wonwell Beach, cross over a little stream leading up to the left of a derelict building. Go over another stile, enter some woodland, and follow the path through it, staying close to the river. Go down some steps to join a partly metalled road leading down to the river. Turn right on to the road, and in about 100 yards up the road, look for a right-pointing sign up the hill and into the woods, signposted 'Kingston 1 mile' (**D**). This is a steep track and can be very muddy and slippery in rain, but it is lovely woodland. As the woodland thins out and before you get to a gate, bear left as indicated by the waymark post. Leave the woods by crossing a stile and keep the hedge to your

immediate right, aiming for a stile on the far side of the field. Cross into the next field and follow the obvious path along the line of the hedge. Go over another stile and into a thorntree-lined path. Over yet another stile, pass into a large arable field where a red arrow mark points diagonally across the field, following the line of a track among the crops, heading towards a flat-topped conifer tree. Where the path meets a bank, bear left. Go through the gap in the next bank where there is the remains of a stile, and continue along the right-hand boundary of the field heading towards a stile and gate. Cross the stile and on to the road. Turn right (**E**) and walk towards Kingston.

The beautiful coastline near Bigbury-on-Sea

When you meet the road in Kingston, turn left, then shortly after turn right passing the Dolphin Inn. At the T-junction, turn left and go on through the village passing the little fire station. Go past the next left and, at the T-junction, turn right at Kingston Plain Cross (**F**). Go on up the hill ignoring the next left. After the road has descended gently downhill for a couple of hundred yards, and then begins to bear more sharply to the left, look for another minor road on the right. Turn right into the unsignposted no through road. Before reaching the buildings of Okenbury, look out on the left for a stile and an open gateway signposted 'Public Footpath to Ringmore 1¼ miles' (**G**).

Head across the field to the right of a little concrete building where there are

three or four stunted trees, and to the right of the gate where there is a footpath-signed stile. Turn left and immediately right following the farm lane downhill, keeping the bank which follows the field boundary on your left. Look out for a low stile in the bank on your left, cross it and follow the left-hand edge of the field. As you reach the bottom of the field, bear right along the lower edge of the field keeping the woodland and steep gully to your left. Watch for a path that dives left down into the woodland — it is yellow arrowed and marked with a public footpath sign. Walk downhill through the trees on a pleasant path which winds its way along the little river valley. You soon come to another stile into a meadow. Cross the field keeping the woodland on your right

and a line of trees along the riverbank to your left. The path can just be seen ahead and soon it becomes more evident as it goes closer to the stream. By the remains of a little castle-like building (**H**), cross a stream, go through the gate, and walk up the muddy lane. Going round a left-hand bend in the lane and within sight of a meadow before a white house, turn right across the field and up to the next stile, crossing another stile in the meantime. Go up the steep grassy meadow to the next stile. Over the stile, turn left and walk towards a gate between a telegraph pole and a fence. Go through the gate and bear right aiming towards another gap in the fence where there is another waymark.

Follow the path as it winds to the left towards a gate to the right of a white house. Just before reaching the gate, look out for a yellow waymark taking you left over a stile and into a narrow footpath. Aim diagonally across the field to the left of a large house towards another stile next to a wall. Go through a narrow kissing gate and turn right on to the village road (**J**). Walk past the pretty little church. Turn right and immediately left as signposted to Challaborough at Ringmore Cross. Pass the post office and, where the signpost points to Challaborough round to the right, go straight on into a 'no through road'. On reaching End House at the end of the lane, go to the left of the house through a gate and head straight on keeping the bank and its wire fence on your immediate right. Descend steeply downhill towards another gate. Go through the gate, turn immediately right by a way post crossing a stile. Go down the hill towards the stream. Climb over the stile and walk across the little stone bridge. Go on up the steep field keeping the hedge to your left. Go through a gate and on to a road (**K**).

Immediately opposite, you will see stone steps leading up to a stile. Cross the stile and go across the field, aiming towards the bank and hedgerow straight ahead up the hill in front of you, after having gone down into the gully. You will soon see a gate ahead with a yellow waymark. Go through the gate and follow the path up beside the hedgebank on your right. Part of the way up the steep climb, go through a gate and keep ascending passing over a stile. As you near the top of the hill, go through another gate and make for a gap in the hedge ahead. Go through the gap and bear a little to the left on to a broad farm track. At a three-way public footpath sign turn right on to a stony track back down to Bigbury-on-Sea. At the bottom of the field go over a stile and back through the houses.

Walk 7
Hound Tor, a medieval village, and Beckaford

Variety is the hallmark of this walk, with delightful woodlands, open moorland, attractive 'in country', and the fascinating remains of a medieval village to add interest. From the higher parts of the moor, the views are breathtaking, although to attain such heights, the climb is also demanding of breath. The tumbled rocks of the tors, especially Bowerman's Nose, allow flights of imagination. Some care is needed in route-finding at the beginning of the walk. Allow about 3 hours.

Begin the walk from **Hound Tor ★** (191) (SX 7479) car park 70 yards from the three-way junction on the road between Widecombe in the Moor ★ and Manaton ★. Walk back to the cross roads and a short distance back up the Widecombe road, until you come to what looks like the beginnings of a tractor track (**A**). Turn left on to the track and walk south-eastwards keeping the rocks of the tor on your left. There is no obvious footpath immediately. Aim a little to the right of a small, solitary tree which is itself to the right of Hound Tor rocks. As you rise slowly up the hill, with the rocky tor some 200 yards to the left, there is a more obvious bridleway through the heather aiming towards a hut circle. On reaching the cyst, where there is also a crossing in the tracks, bear half left keeping Hound Tor rocks still to your left and head up over the hill. On the horizon a little to the right can clearly be seen the prominent outcrop of Haytor Rocks. At the top of the hill, with Hound Tor rocks immediately to the left, you can see the rocks of Greator ahead, and you aim

The site of the Medieval village at Hound Tor.

slightly to the left of them. Go down the hill towards the gap in a boundary wall. Pass the intriguing remains of the medieval village as you go down hill (**B**).

Continue on through a gap in the next field boundary and follow the main track on up towards a gate, which can be seen ahead, keeping Greator rocks on the right and woodland on the left. This is fine Dartmoor-edge countryside. Follow the public bridlepath through the gate heading towards Leighon via Haytor Down. Go on down the track and through a gate. Go through another hunting gate and continue on down the broad track. Pass between two stone posts and step across the small rivulet. Cross the main stream on a small clapper bridge and go on up some stony steps through old birch woodland among rounded, moss- and lichen-covered boulders. Emerging from the wood, the track continues on uphill. Rising up the hill and out of the wood, you will come to a wooden signpost waymarked with a blue spot to the left towards Leighon. Follow this track avoiding any diversions to right or left keeping the bulk of the wood on the left. Just before reaching the boundary wall ahead with a fence behind it, bear right on the narrow track up hill. Keeping a stone wall on your left, aim at a gap between the left-hand stone wall and another coming from the right ahead. As the walls almost touch, there is another wooden signpost leading you through a gate and down a bridle track between stone walls. To the left are the rocky outcrops of Greator and Hound Tor. Pass through another gate. Continue down the track towards the boundary fence of a white house and bear right going uphill (**C**).

Continue on uphill following the sign indicating 'Public Bridlepath Upper Terrace Drive'. Pass through another gate and carry on up the lane. As you ascend the hill, on the slopes to the left you will see the houses of Manaton with the church keeping watch over the village. You are

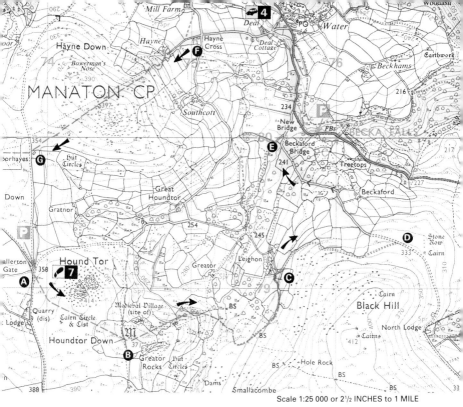

now on a good farm lane. You soon emerge on to a minor road (**D**) where you turn left. Go through the gate or over the cattle grid. The narrow winding road heads steeply down hill towards Beckaford Bridge (**E**). Go over the little stone road bridge and pause a moment to gaze at this lovely stream burbling through old flower-filled birch woods. Pass the private drive of Leighon. At the T-junction turn left at Leighon Cross signposted to Manaton. Although this could be a busy road, especially at the height of the tourist season, the damp woodlands on either side are most attractive with marsh marigolds, primroses, and other wild flowers growing in profusion. In summer there are yellow flags. Pass over another pretty little brook and you soon approach the houses of Freeland on the outskirts of Manaton (on **Tour 4**).

Just before the post office of Manaton Stores, turn left, signposted to Southcott, immediately opposite the Kestor Inn. Crossing another little stream, the road then rises ahead. At Hayne Cross (**F**) continue straight across the road on to another lane signposted and blue dotted towards Hayne Down, Jay's Grave, and Natsworthy Gate. This is a public bridleway with 'no through road for vehicles'.

Where the metalled road peters out and becomes a gravel track, with a gravel drive to a house to the right, continue on up the muddy lane. Reaching the end of the woodland, go through a gate and follow the clearly defined track uphill. Soon a path goes off to the right following a wall but you should continue onwards. Shortly after, the way divides with one fork going up towards a rocky outcrop; go straight ahead on the left fork. Keep on the bouldery track uphill with the rocky outcrops off to your right. On the skyline ahead, there is a small, pointed, triangular rock to which you should aim and to which the track will take you. Pause for breath here and take in the wonderful views of Devonshire countryside behind including Manaton and its church. From this side, you will be unable to see it but, on the far side of the rocky outcrop to the right, there is the oddly shaped rock called Bowerman's Nose which you will be able to see behind you further down the hill the other side.

On reaching the brow of the hill the moorland opens up before you and behind there are simply beautiful views. Go over the hill and down the other side towards the road with the rocks of Hound Tor clearly visible ahead and to the left. From here you can just see your car park. On reaching the metalled road (**G**), turn left and go through Moyle's Gate to continue along the road back to the car park. Look back towards the rocks here and you will clearly see Bowerman's Nose to the left of the main part of the rocky tor.

Walk 8
King's Oven and the Two Moors Way

This is quite a long and, in places, arduous walk including moorland, 'in country', and some interesting navigation across open fields and through farmyards. Anyone who is nervous of farm stock should not attempt this walk unless accompanied by someone used to such animals. There are also places where dogs may have to be lifted over stiles, and others where the mud can be deep.

Begin the walk in the car park about 100 yards to the north-east of the Warren House Inn. This is King's Oven, on **Tour 8**, and the walk starts by following the track a little south of east heading towards the disused shaft, the river, and Headland Warren. Continue on the broad, rough track downwards a little more to the south until it reaches the stream at the bottom of the valley. Before reaching the stream, however, where the broad track veers to the left, take the right-hand fork down a rough path towards the stream. Cross the stream by the small stone footbridge (**A**) and follow the slightly indistinct track forking

only a little to the right. Do not be tempted to turn right along the track by the river.

Head up the hill, keeping the round mound of the moorland ahead. As you climb, keep the stone wall on your right and follow the rough track in a narrow gully. Carry on up towards the pass between the hills. The path veers a little to the left as you climb, following the shallow gully on the left. As you reach the brow of the hill the gully is now to the right. Go over the hill and descend the other side. Where the path forks with one fork going to the right towards Headland Warren Farm, our way takes us to the left continuing on past the farm (**B**). The path then snakes to the left and continues uphill towards the road where you turn right. After about ½ mile, before reaching a sharp right turn in the road at Firth Bridge, a path leaves the road to the left where there are some stone steps to act as a waymark (**C**).

Follow the broad track uphill once again along the line of a small stream. Cross a little stream and you will soon enter the enclosure wall of Grimspound. There is a broad track to the left to the top of Hookney Tor but walk on through the pound a little north of east. A little over ½ mile beyond Grimspound fork to the right. At an apparent crossroads as you descend the hill, continue straight on the main track. Follow the path down the hill with the wood-

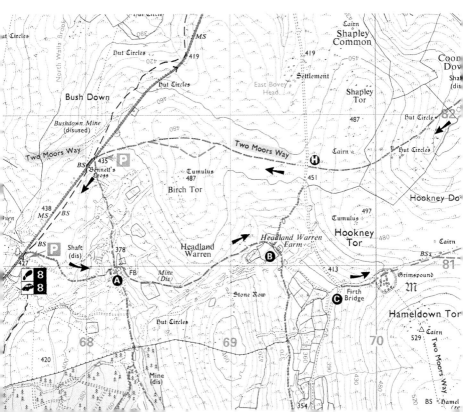

land to the left and the East Webburn River to the right. Just before reaching the little stream and the gate out on to a narrow road turn sharp left over a gate into the woodland (**D**). If you reach the footpath marker, it is signposted towards Moor Gate. The track through the woodland is waymarked with yellow dots and yellow arrows but you should follow the instructions carefully.

Continue heading northwards through the wood. Just before reaching Heathercombe, enter the clearing through a gate and continue on straight ahead towards the house. Emerging on to a narrow road, cross it, and follow the public footpath sign to Moor Gate. Follow the track uphill through another gated way into the woodland once more. Having crossed the gate, at an apparent crossroads in the ways, take the right fork following the yellow arrow and dots, on a grassy woodland path. At the next fork where one track goes downhill and straight on, your way goes to the left at first, following the yellow arrows. Almost immediately after, there is another fork at which you turn right. Continue to be guided by the yellow waymarks. At the end of the wood, there is a stiled gate. Cross the stile and continue straight on towards the next gate. Cross a little stream at this point.

Keeping the buildings of Kendon Farm

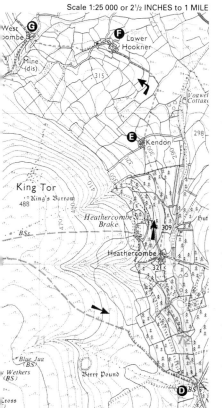

Scale 1:25 000 or 2¹/₂ INCHES to 1 MILE

(**E**) on your left, cross the road through the yellow-marked gate. Go diagonally across the field to the next gate which has a waymarked stone gatepost. Go through into a grassy meadow. Aim diagonally across the meadow towards a line of trees, and on the far side of the next meadow there is a gate to which you should head. Cross a little stream and in the corner of the field cross a stile. Shortly after the stile, the path turns to the left through a stiled gate and into a narrow, grassy, gated lane. Walk on down the lane towards Lower Hookner (**F**). Pass through a gate and into the farmyard. Turn right in front of the farmhouse and continue through the farmyard going out of the next gate following the yellow waymark. Emerging from the farmyard, in front of some old stone barns, turn left heading up the hill along a farm lane. Soon after, look out for a gate on the right marked with the yellow dot. Go through the gate and follow the right of way on the left-hand edge of the field keeping the boundary on your immediate left. Go to the next gate by the left-hand edge of the field which is also waymarked. Turn a-third right across the next field towards another gate also with its yellow spot on the stone gatepost, crossing a little stream just before the gate. Aim at the gap in the field boundary directly opposite the gate.

Go through the next stone-posted gap in the bank heading towards the farm buildings of King's Barrow at West Coombe (**G**), and a stile on the far side of the field. Go over the stile over the next field boundary and bear half right to a gap in the wall beside the stream. Cross the stream on some stepping stones and walk straight on into the centre of the farm buildings turning left, and following the bridle path to the moor. Where the track forks to the right to a house, veer left and the heights of King Tor rise up on the left-hand side.

Continue following the well-defined bridle track across the moor. Carry on up the hill following the broader of the various tracks heading towards the jagged stones of a hut circle. Go through their remains and carry on up the hill towards the stone wall ahead. Go through the gate and, as you reach a broad crossing path, turn left and on reaching the next broken wall of a field boundary, turn right following the track downhill and keeping the stone wall on the left. Cross the minor road (**H**) on to the footpath bearing very slightly to the right and follow the distinctive sometimes slightly sunken path across the open moorland. Go over the top of the hill and past the cairn. Go down to the road and turn left back to the car park.

Walk 9
Bellever Forest and around Laughter Tor

This walk gives you the opportunity to enjoy pleasant forest walking and some open moorland where there is a real sense of space and remoteness. Apart from the stretches of the walk between points B and C and F and G, where route-finding could be a little tricky, especially in mist weather, this is an easy walk. Much of the route is on Forestry Commission tracks which are broad, fairly level, and partly gravelled or metalled. There is a variety of forest walks in Bellever Forest, some of which would be suitable for wheel chair users. Allow 2-2½ hours.

Park in the National Park Information Centre car park at Postbridge ★ (191) (SX 647789). Turn left out of the car park and walk down the road for a short distance passing the post office stores on your left-hand side. Just before the road bridge on the B3212 crossing the East Dart River, and a few yards from the splendid clapper bridge, turn right on to a public bridlepath signposted to Bellever (**A**). Follow the obvious bridletrack, keeping the river on your left.

Go through another hunting gate and the bridlepath takes you uphill on an uneven rocky track which then becomes a grassy way across the moorland edge country. The East Dart River is now down in the valley to your left. Continue onwards keeping the drystone wall to your immediate left. Pass a small plantation on your left-hand side and a more major arm of the Bellever Forest ★ on the right. You can now see what looks like a minor road more or less straight ahead. It is in fact a Forestry Commission unmetalled road, and you soon join it. Continue on up the road bearing to the right.

Shortly before the forest road meets the minor road leading down into Bellever (**B**), fork off to the left on a reasonably obvious track across the grassland. The right of way now runs roughly parallel with the road keeping it just a short distance to your right. The obvious track, however, actually seems to join the road itself. As you pass over the hill, the roofs of the first houses which mark the hamlet of Bellever come into view. Just to the left of the houses ahead, you can see Bellever Bridge crossing the East Dart.

Pass a post box by the side of the road and cross over a little stream. Where the road bears sharply to the right and crosses a cattle grid, go through a hunting gate to the left of the cattle grid (**C**) and continue straight across the rocky patch of grassland aiming for a wooden bridlepath sign and a Forestry Commission sign to its left. Cross the road and enter the forest following the sign Public Bridlepath to 'Laughter Hole Farm and County Road B3357 at Huccaby Cottage'. You are now following a gravelled Forestry Commission road.

Although this is old coniferous forest, the smell of the pine resin does, to some extent, make up for the lack of understorey and, in spring, there is still plenty of bird song. Walk on through the Forestry Commission parking area where there are toilets open during the main tourist season. Continue following the route that is now signposted 'Forest Walk'. Soon, the 'Forest Walk' signs point to the right but follow the old public bridleway sign which now points straight ahead and uphill towards a hunting gate. Go through the gate and continue on up following the direction indicated by the old wooden 'PATH' sign. Through the trees on your left, you can catch glimpses of the East Dart River down in the valley below. The bridle road now ascends a little once again.

Soon after you arrive over the brow of the first hill, the road goes straight ahead on up the hill towards the skyline. At this there is a fork signposted to Laughter Hole House to the left and Laughter Hole Farm to the right. Follow the bridlepath to the right towards Laughter Hole Farm.

Where the Forestry Commission road makes a sharp turning back on itself to the right and into the wood, continue following the path straight ahead and pass through a gate bearing the sign of 'Laughter Hole Farm'. Continue on along the farm track. Pass by the collection of old farm buildings and go through the next gate where the farmhouse itself can be seen on your right — a more recent-looking, white-painted bungalow.

The track forks here with one fork to the left signposted 'Bridle Path to Sherill 1½ miles, Stepping Stones and Babeny'. There is also another track going down to the left to what presumably is Laughter Hole House but that is not a public right of way. Your route, however, goes uphill on the bridlepath signposted 'County Road B3357 at Huccaby Cottage' (**D**).

Just before you reach the top of the slope, you come to a wooden signpost indicating that your way carries straight on towards a pair of gates and another wooden signpost. Go through the gate and continue straight on, this time sign-posted 'Public Bridlepath to Dunnabridge Pound' (**E**). Do not take the left-hand route signposted to the B3357.

As you reach the highest part of this section of the walk, look out on the right-hand side of the track for the obvious evidence of a stone row. Shortly after you have passed the stone row, another wooden signpost comes into view ahead. Pass between the stone posts of the boundary wall. Unless you are planning to visit Dunnabridge Pound down in the valley straight ahead, turn right here (**F**) where the the public bridlepath signpost points to Bellever Tor. At first, however, there is no obvious sign of a track, but just keep walking in the direction indicated by the signpost until you go over the hill and you can see the rocky heights of Bellever Tor ahead. Aim towards the tor. The low tor to your right is Laughter Tor, the other side of which is Laughter Hole Farm which you passed by earlier.

Continue aiming roughly towards the tor itself, although it is as well to make slightly to its left where you can see a wall from the right joining another wall at right-angles and where you can just make out a wooden signpost and a gate. To the right of that, and just below Bellever Tor. three walls meet and you can see another wooden signpost. When you reach the gate (**G**), notice it has been marked with a yellow spot. Go through the gate and turn right following the line of the wall on your right. You soon reach the point where the three walls meet, and you should follow the direction indicated by the footpath sign, going slightly uphill and heading roughly towards Bellever Tor. Continue on towards the forest keeping the wall on your immediate right and the tor on your left.

At a three-way signpost just before reaching the forest (**H**), turn left up the hill keeping the forest on your right. Follow the footpath on the left-hand edge of the forest, and you are guided by marker posts with red bands. The path then meets a boundary wall where the post with a red spot on it, the red banded route, takes you into the forest (**J**). You then come to a crossing of the ways, and your route continues straight on signposted to Postbridge. You are here crossing the route of the Lichway ★.

Continue to follow the woodland road which is now gravelled and partly metalled. Although there are those who may find walking along these broad tracks through Forestry Commission plantations a little dull, its is tranquil, fragrant, and the air is filled with bird song in spring —

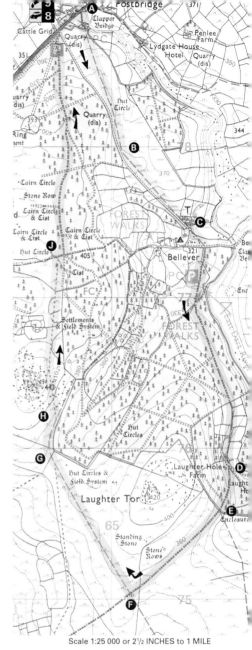

Scale 1:25 000 or 2½ INCHES to 1 MILE

especially the calls of the tiny goldcrests.

Where another Forestry Commission road enters from the right, simply continue straight on into what is now younger plantation. The forest road now descends towards Postbridge. As you reach the bottom of the hill, not far from the road, go through another hunting gate and continue on down towards the road. Bear left on to a minor road and cross a cattle grid to emerge on to the B3212 where you turn right and the car park is immediately on your left.

125

Walk 10
The East and West Dart Rivers

Like many walks in South Devon, this one has its attractions and its problems. It involves crossing the East Dart River on a well-built stepping stone bridge; the West Dart has to be crossed by stepping stones, too, but the stones are uneven and, after rain, may be below the water's level. From Badger's Holt to Rogues Roost, the path is indistinct although it is easy enough to see which way to go and it would also be possible to stay by the river for much of the way. And between Week Ford and the point where the route turns north back to Dartmeet, the path again peters out. There are refreshment facilities and a gift shop at Dartmeet. Allow 2-3 hours.

Begin the walk from the large free car park at the popular tourist spot of **Dartmeet ★** (191) (SX 6773) on **Tour 4**. At the Badger's Holt end of the car park on the right, pass through a gate at the right of the main entrance to Badger's Holt. This is signposted to Cator Gate via Sherwell or Sherril. You are on a well-defined path ascending gently uphill veering away a little from the river. Just at the back of the buildings where the most obvious path seems to go down to the river, take a path uphill to the right (**A**). This is quite steep. On reaching a grassy clearing, by a gnarled old thorn tree and a collapsed wall, the way continues up the hill towards Yar Tor. By a small group of five old thorn trees, bear leftish and pick up the narrow track contouring a little up the hill. Eventually, the track becomes more evident among the heathery tussocks, and is more or less parallel with the river valley below and with the rocky outcrop of Yar Tor above you on the right. This is tussocky, heathery, bouldery country but there is a path which seems to pick its way through.

Shortly before the river below turns away to the left, and with some houses ahead and a group of trees below you, the path veers a little to the left heading towards a gate in the boundary wall ahead. Cross the gate and stile, and continue down through the meadow keeping the field boundary immediately on your left. Yellow arrows on the gates help to identify the route. At the bottom corner of the field go through a narrow gate with its yellow arrow and dot. Carry on down to the narrow wooden footbridge. Cross the bridge and its accompanying stile and head across

the marshy ground to the gate opposite. The ground here can be quite boggy. Go through the gate into the next meadow and follow the direction indicated by the Public Footpath signpost. You can now just see the yellow waymark on a post on the other side of the field to the right of a telegraph post. Go over the low wall and stile and ahead there is a forking road to the left (**B**). Take the first, left, or lower fork. Follow this road round in front of the large white-painted house and the drive to Rogue's Roost Cottage. Continue on the road for about 500 yards and, before it makes a sharp turn right towards Babeny, immediately before the little stream, turn left on to a public bridleway with a blue waymark.

Blue dots on rocks also mark the way half-right across the meadow towards the stream. Do not be tempted to follow a track up the hill. Go across a damp, grassy meadow. It may not be easy to cross the stream on the recommended stepping stones if the water is high and you may need to walk upstream until a suitable crossing point is found. Once you have crossed the stream and walked towards its junction with the East Dart, you then need to cross the river on the splendid stepping stone bridge (**C**). Turn left down the bank of the river. Shortly the path veers away from the river a little and up towards some coniferous trees. Go through a gate and keep to the right of the meadow aiming towards a gap in the stone wall ahead. Go through the gap by the remains of an old building and head straight across the next meadow to the obvious gap in the boundary opposite. Follow the broad, reddish farm track going gently up the hill away from the river. The farm lane is blue waymarked at regular intervals. As you climb, there are good views of the moors over to the left with the river quite a long way below now.

Passing through a gate you will soon arrive at Brimpts Farm and the public footpath turns right before reaching the farm and then very soon left, passing through two gates. Go through another gate into the farmyard and walk on down the lane. It then becomes a concreted causeway and you bear right rather than going left into the farm itself. There are dining rooms, garden tables, cream teas, toilets, and parking to be found here. Where the lane forks sharply left, carry straight on as the blue waymarks indicate, passing into a plantation. Go out on to the road (**D**) via a gate and cattle grid. Turn right if you are continuing the walk, or you could turn left for a short cut back down to the car. Continuing on the walk, you soon come to a left turning signposted to Hexworthy. Go down the narrow road and, in a little over 500 yards, just before Huccaby Farm, turn left on to a farm track.

You will soon see a wooden signpost blue waymarked to the right 'Bridlepath to the Road near Combstone Tor'. Go through a blue waymarked gate into a lane. Now just follow the blue-marked bridlepath. To the right can be seen one of the meanders of the East Dart River. Go on down towards the river, passing between stone walls further on, and bearing gradually left. You soon reach the river at Week Ford (**E**) where there are stepping stones. Having crossed the river, bear left as indicated by the signpost and the blue waymark on the tree. Cross another small rivulet and go over a footbridge. At a three-way signpost, go through the gate following the direction for the bridle path to Holne Moor. Turn right at first following the wire fence on the right for a short distance, then by a concrete marker, bear left following a track up through the bouldery bank where orange dots can just be made out on the rocks and trees.

Follow the indistinct path as the dots and two-way arrows indicate. Go around some boggy ground aiming for a gap in the wall ahead. Go through or over the stone stile following the path upwards and aiming for a gap in the next wall. Bear half left towards a gate in the next wall and follow the well-marked track to the left heading uphill, between two low, but upright stones. There is a gully on the right here. You soon reach another three-way signpost (**F**) and you need to go left signposted to Dartmeet Stepping Stones. You are now on a gravel farm track. Where the gravel track turns right across a cattle grid towards a house, you turn left down the bridlepath towards Dartmeet. Just keep the boundary wall on your right and descend through sheep-grazing meadows. When you come to a wired-off plantation, bear left and head down to the river and the stepping stones which you must cross once more before climbing up past the house to the road and the Dartmeet car park.

Scale 1:25 000 or 2½ INCHES to 1 MILE

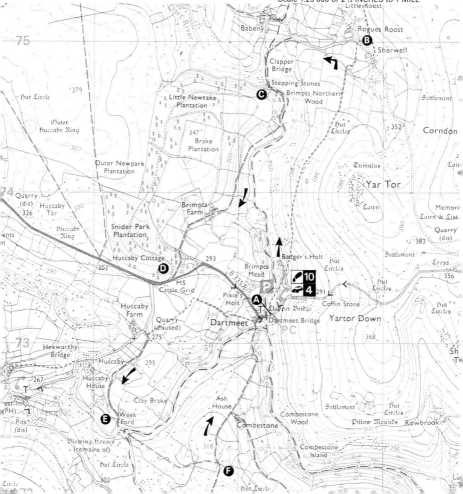

Walk 11
The Walkham Valley

Although there are one or two places where the going can be muddy and churned by horses after rain, this is a delightful walk, especially in spring or early summer when there is bird song to accompany you and when flowers line the charming Devon lanes. At the start of the walk, the granite quarry is soon lost to view, and you are immersed in some lovely countryside. It is worth noting that there are two car parks to the east of Merrivale, and it makes sense to park in the one nearer the inn, to shorten the walk on the B3357 road. Allow 3-4 hours.

Park in the Merrivale car park on the B3357 in sight of the quarry workings and the Dartmoor Inn. From the car park walk down the road past the Inn and the quarry. Go over the new road bridge at Merrivale (191) (SX 5475) on **Tour 8** and on past the inn. Walk on up the road past the entrance to Merrivale Farm on the left and Dartmoor Granite Co. on the right. Rising up the hill, and where the stone wall leaves the road to the left and you come across the Grimstone and Sortridge Leat, take the left path running parallel to the leat for a short distance (**A**). Keep the leat on your right and follow the line of a stone wall on the left. There is a path of sorts over bouldery, grassy country. Where the leat veers away to the right (west), your route continues straight ahead in a roughly south-westerly direction. Soon, the upstanding rocks of Vixen Tor come into view. The now broad bridletrack veers a little to the left as you pass the tor and heads downhill towards the stream. The track continues past the point where the stone wall makes a right-angled bend to the left, and then heads a little to the right of it towards the stream with the tor now behind you.

Cross the little stream, bearing half-left and aiming towards another stream where you can just make out the track on the other side. Cross this stream by some stepping stones (**B**) and head up the hill keeping the boundary wall well to the left, aiming towards the point where the left-hand boundary wall seems to come to an end. Continue on between the low broken rocks of Heckwood Tor and the wall to the left. Here the track becomes a broader, rough lane. Pass the remains of Heckwood Quarry where you can clearly see the worked granite blocks. Continue on the broad track across the moorland keeping the boundary wall on your left. In the

distance you can see the tower of Sampford Spiney church; on the right there is a lonely white house with Pew Tor at its back. The track joins the gravel drive of the Pewtor Cottage and you continue on towards the tower of the church keeping the wall of the house's garden on your immediate right. On reaching a minor road which is a cul-de-sac to the right, cross it, and go on following the footpath sign. You rejoin a minor road and carry on in the same direction passing a little fork and clapper bridge into Eastontown. (**C**)

Just past a cattle grid and before another group of buildings, where the road turns sharp right, look out for a small wooden footpath sign pointing you to the left. Go through a gate and into the farmyard. At the back of the farm buildings where there are three gates, take the centre gate where it is signposted 'footpath'. Head up the hill following the muddy tractor track towards a point where a line of trees becomes gradually lower and meets a line of bushes. Go through the gap in the field boundary right in the corner where the yellow waymark on a stone post shows the way. Head diagonally across the field towards a stile. Cross the stile and bear half-right towards a laddered stile on the bank. Walk on keeping the coppiced thorns on top of the wall to your immediate right, and shortly, go through another gap into the next field. Follow the indistinct track running parallel to the right-hand field boundary. By a small woodland where there is a corrugated iron shed, go through a gate and pass into a wall-bounded lane. Go on down the lane which becomes grassy as it passes the fine stone house of 'Stonycroft'.

Go through the gate at the end of the lane and on to a minor road. Turn sharp left down the stony lane. You soon arrive at another road where there is a cattle grid and hunting gate, and you turn left. Go on down the road and then cross the pretty River Walkham by the attractive stone Ward Bridge (**D**) and go on up the steep hill. Nearing the top of the hill, at Cript Tor Cross, turn left signposted to Daveytown. Although this is a tarmac lane, on a fine day particularly in spring or early summer, it makes for very pleasant walking as you follow the line of the Walkham valley. Pass the lane leading to Withill and cross the little stream — a most attractive brook spanned by a lovely bridge. It tumbles through the woodland among the great moss- and lichen-covered granite boulders. In spring the air is alive with the song of willow warblers, chiffchaffs, blackbirds, and songthrushes. Pass the narrow lane to Parktown on the left and go on up

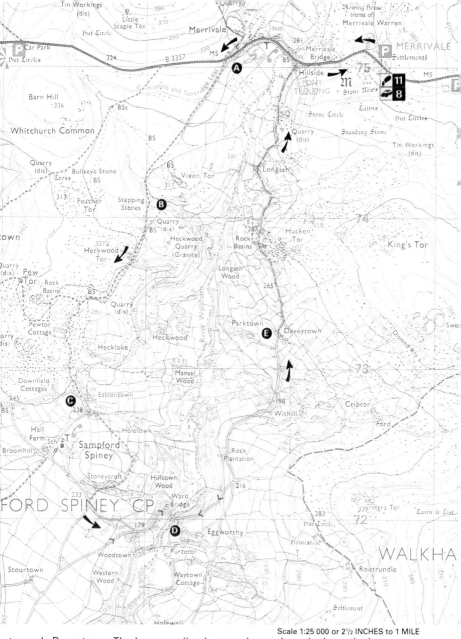

Scale 1:25 000 or 2½ INCHES to 1 MILE

towards Daveytown. The lanes are lined with celandines, stitchwort, honesty, wood sorrel, violets, primroses, bluebells, and the round leaves of navelwort clinging to the walls. At the little collection of houses which comprises Daveytown (**E**), go on up the stony lane as indicated by the wooden signpost pointing to Merrivale 1½ miles. Go through two gates and continue up the lane. Go through another gate. Bar the noise from an occasional passing aircraft, the silence is broken only by the kronking of ravens in the valley to the left.

Pass through another gate in the lane by the perched formations of Hucken Tor. As you descend gently down the lane, passing the tor, it seems that all too soon, you can see the workings of Merrivale Quarry ahead while to the left there is another fine view, this time from a different angle, of Vixen Tor. Cross a tributary to the River Walkham rushing down the hillside from the right. Go over a little bridge. Follow the bridle track through the gates past Longash and walk through the farmyard. Carry on up the tarmac lane as indicated by the blue waymarks. Go through another gate at Hillside Riding Centre. On reaching the road, turn right to walk back to the car park.

Walk 12
Sheepstor, Ditsworthy Warren, and Ringmoor Down

Of all the walks on Dartmoor described in this book, this one best conjures an aura of lonely moor and a sense of prehistory. The complex of stone rows and cairns in Drizzle Combe are testament to a great deal of human activity here some four or five thousand years ago. Looking for all the world like a setting for a Daphne DuM Maurier novel, Ditsworthy Warren House, seems far too grand to have been a warrener's house, but the area certainly gets its name from the rabbit warrening which was carried on here from Norman times. Unless you are skilled in the use of map and compass, do not attempt this walk in poor visibility. Allow 2-3 hours.

Park on the grassy area a little to the north of Ringmoor Cottage on Portland Lane at the viewpoint overlooking Burrator Reservoir. Walk on up the road with the village of **Sheepstor** (202) (SX 5567) ahead and a little to the left. From here there are panoramic views across Sheep's Tor, Burrator Reservoir, and the 'in-country' as well as to the church of Sheepstor. Although this is walking on a minor road, the views all around certainly make up for it. At the T-junction (**A**) where, down the hill to the left

is Sheepstor, turn right on to the unsign-posted minor road heading slightly uphill. Pass Gutter Tor on the right before reaching a small stand of coniferous trees. Pass a track to the right which winds up past Gutter Tor, and you soon come to a ford across the stream before which there is alternative car parking space. On the other side of the stream, go on up the stony track passing the coniferous plantation. In the plantation there is a gate to the right where a scout hut can just be seen among the

Scale 1:25 000 or 2½ INCHES to 1 MILE

A panoramic view across Sheep's Tor towards Burrator Reservoir and Sheepstor Church.

trees. It would be possible to turn right here (**B**) on to Edward's Path as a short cut but the full route continues on up the hill.

Cross a little stone bridge, and there is now a real sense of space as you walk across the open, rolling, grassy moorland. Where the going begins to level out, you can can see Higher Hartor Tor ahead and a little to the right. Where the path begins to descend, and just beyond the point where three low granite posts approach your path, turn right at a fork or continue on a little then turning hard right and back on yourself (**C**). If you have taken the first right fork, you will come to what looks like another fork just before going down to some wet ground and a brook. There is also the remains of a boundary wall here. Turn right keeping the Drizzle Combe Brook on your left. As you head downhill, you can see the remains of a settlement. You are now on a fairly distinct, broad, grassy track heading downhill in Ditsworthy Warren with the stream on your left. Cross the small leat, and then bear a little to the right still keeping the main stream on your left. Look for the standing stones on the far side of the stream to your left. At a point before a low rocky mound ahead, where a right fork seems to take you to a solitary standing stone, bear left heading a little to the left of the low mound. There seem to be leats and standing stones everywhere here so there is a strong sense of history and prehistory. Look for the rocky outcrop of Shavercombe Tor on the other side of the valley to the left. Just before reaching the lower slopes of Eastern Tor, the path becomes much more obvious again as a broad gravelly packhorse trail. You soon reach the lonely grey building of Ditsworthy Warren House (**D**).

Pass the house on your left. The windows are now blinded and its entrance is barred but it looks down the valley ahead, and only the horses, sheep, and a lonely buzzard are here to enjoy the moor. Walk down what seems to be the main drive to the house, pass by a small pool in a hollow before rising up the hill ahead and follow one of the various tracks up the hill to a fence and a gate where there is a public footpath signpost as you near the top of the hill. Continue straight on along the public bridlepath heading towards the road near Ringmoor Cottage. Once again, you are walking across, broad, open, rolling, grassy moorland. Follow the hoof-marked broad track over the hill keeping an enclosed, bright-green-looking area of pasture to the left. Arriving down near Ringmoor Cottage, turn right on to the road and walk back up the hill to the car.

CONVENTIONAL SIGNS 1:250 000 or 1 INCH to 4 MILES

ROADS
Not necessarily rights of way

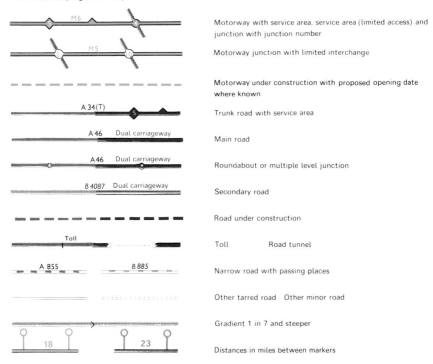

Motorway with service area, service area (limited access) and junction with junction number

Motorway junction with limited interchange

Motorway under construction with proposed opening date where known

Trunk road with service area

Main road

Roundabout or multiple level junction

Secondary road

Road under construction

Toll   Road tunnel

Narrow road with passing places

Other tarred road   Other minor road

Gradient 1 in 7 and steeper

Distances in miles between markers

The representation of a road is no evidence of the existence of a right of way

PRIMARY ROUTES

These form a national network of recommended through routes which complement the motorway system.
Selected places of major traffic importance are known as Primary Route Destinations and are shown thus **EXETER**
Distances and directions to such destinations are repeated on traffic signs which, on primary routes, have a green background or, on motorways, have a blue background.
To continue on a primary route through or past a place which has appeared as a destination on previous signs, follow the directions to the next primary destination shown on the green-backed signs.

RAILWAYS

Standard gauge track

Narrow gauge track

Tunnel

Road crossing under or over

Level crossing

Station

WATER FEATURES

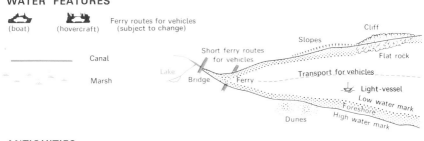

(boat)   (hovercraft)   Ferry routes for vehicles (subject to change)

Canal

Marsh

Cliff

Slopes

Flat rock

Short ferry routes for vehicles

Lake

Bridge   Ferry

Transport for vehicles

Light-vessel

Low water mark

Foreshore

High water mark

Dunes

ANTIQUITIES

✳ Native fortress   ∧ Site of battle (with date)   Roman road (course of)   CANOVIUM • Roman antiquity

Castle •   Other antiquities

𝔪   Ancient Monuments and Historic Buildings in the care of the Secretaries of State for the Environment, for Scotland and for Wales and that are open to the public.

BOUNDARIES

+ ― + ― + ― + ― National

― ― ― ― ― ― ― { County, Region
or Islands Area

GENERAL FEATURES

Buildings

Wood

Lighthouse (in use)

Lighthouse (disused)

Windmill

Radio or TV mast

▲ Youth hostel

⊕ Civil aerodrome { with Customs facilities

✦ { without Customs facilities

Ⓗ Heliport

✆ Public telephone

✆ Motoring organisation telephone

+ Intersection, latitude & longitude at 30' intervals (not shown where it confuses important detail)

TOURIST INFORMATION

✝ Abbey, Cathedral, Priory

🐟 Aquarium

⋏ Camp site

🚐 Caravan site

🏰 Castle

Cave

Country park

Craft centre

Garden

Golf course or links

Historic house

Information centre

Motor racing

Museum

Nature or forest trail

Nature reserve

☆ Other tourist feature

✕ Picnic site

Preserved railway

Racecourse

Skiing

Viewpoint

Wildlife park

Zoo

WALKS, CYCLE & MOTOR TOURS
Applicable to all scales

🖋1 Start point of walk

➜ Route of walk

Featured walk

🚗1 Start point of tour

➜ Route of tour

Featured tour

Start point of mini-walk

Featured mini-walk

FOLLOW THE COUNTRY CODE
Enjoy the countryside and respect its life and work

Guard against all risk of fire

Fasten all gates

Keep your dogs under close control

Keep to public paths across farmland

Leave livestock, crops and machinery alone

Use gates and stiles to cross fences, hedges and walls

Take your litter home

Help to keep all water clean

Protect wildlife, plants and trees

Take special care on country roads

Make no unnecessary noise

CONVENTIONAL SIGNS
1:25 000 or 2½ INCHES to 1 MILE

ROADS AND PATHS

Not necessarily rights of way

M I or A 6(M)	M I or A 6(M)	Motorway
A 31 (T)	A 31(T)	Trunk road
A 35	A 35	Main road
B 3074	B 3074	Secondary road
A 35	A 35	Dual carriageway

Narrow roads with passing places are annotated

Road generally more than 4m wide

Road generally less than 4m wide

Other road, drive or track

Unfenced roads and tracks are shown by pecked lines

Path

PUBLIC RIGHTS OF WAY

Public rights of way may not be evident on the ground

- - - - - - - } Public paths { Footpath / Bridleway

+ + + + + Byway open to all traffic

Road used as a public path

The indication of a towpath in this book does not necessarily imply a public right of way
The representation of any other road, track or path is no evidence of the existence of a right of way

BOUNDARIES

— · — · — · — County (England and Wales)

— — — — — District

—·—·—·— London Borough

· · · · · · · · · · · Civil Parish (England)* Community (Wales)

— — — — — — — Constituency (County, Borough, Burgh or European Assembly)

Coincident boundaries are shown by the first appropriate symbol

*For Ordnance Survey purposes County Boundary is deemed to be the limit of the parish structure whether or not a parish area adjoins

RAILWAYS

Multiple track } Standard gauge

Single track

Narrow gauge

Siding

Cutting

Embankment

Tunnel

Road over & under

Level crossing; station

DANGER AREA

MOD ranges in the area
Danger!
Observe warning notices

Mountain Rescue Post

SYMBOLS

♦ Church or ▲ chapel +	with tower / with spire / without tower or spire	
▨ △	Glasshouse; youth hostel	
⬳	Bus or coach station	
⚓ ⚓ ⚓	Lighthouse; lightship; beacon	
△	Triangulation station	
Triangulation point on	church or chapel / lighthouse, beacon / building; chimney	

pylon · pole Electricity transmission line

VILLA Roman antiquity (AD 43 to AD 420)

Castle Other antiquities

⊹ Site of antiquity

⚔ 1066 Site of battle (with date)

Gravel pit

Sand pit

Chalk pit, clay pit or quarry

Refuse or slag heap

Sloping wall

[ ] Water   [ ] Mud

[ ] Sand; sand & shingle

National Park or Forest Park Boundary

NT National Trust always open

NT National Trust opening restricted

FC Forestry Commission

VEGETATION
Limits of vegetation are defined by positioning of the symbols but may be delineated also by pecks or dots

Coniferous trees

Non-coniferous trees

Coppice

Orchard

Scrub

Bracken, rough grassland

In some areas bracken ( ) and rough grassland ( ) are shown separately } Shown collectively as rough grassland on some sheets

Heath

Reeds

Marsh

Saltings

HEIGHTS AND ROCK FEATURES

50 · } Determined { ground survey
285 · } by { air survey

Surface heights are to the nearest metre above mean sea level. Heights shown close to a triangulation pillar refer to the station height at ground level and not necessarily to the summit

Vertical face

75
60
50

Loose rock Boulders Outcrop Scree

Contours are at 5 metres vertical interval

ABBREVIATIONS
1:25 000 or 2½ INCHES to 1 MILE also 1:10 000/1:10 560 or 6 INCHES to 1 MILE

BP,BS	Boundary Post or Stone	P	Post Office	A,R	Telephone, AA or RAC
CH	Club House	Pol Sta	Police Station	TH	Town Hall
F V	Ferry Foot or Vehicle	PC	Public Convenience	Twr	Tower
FB	Foot Bridge	PH	Public House	W	Well
HO	House	Sch	School	Wd Pp	Wind Pump
MP,MS	Mile Post or Stone	Spr	Spring		
Mon	Monument	T	Telephone, public		

Abbreviations applicable only to 1:10 000/1:10 560 or 6 INCHES to 1 MILE

Ch	Church	GP	Guide Post	TCB	Telephone Call Box
F Sta	Fire Station	P	Pole or Post	TCP	Telephone Call Post
Fn	Fountain	S	Stone	Y	Youth Hostel

Maps and Mapping

Most early maps of the area covered by this guide were published on a county basis, and, if you wish to follow their development in detail, R. V. Tooley's *Maps and Map Makers* will be found most useful. The first significant county maps were produced by Christopher Saxton in the 1570s, the whole of England and Wales being covered in only six years. Although he did not cover the whole country, John Norden, working at the end of the sixteenth century, was the first map-maker to show roads. In 1611-12, John Speed, making use of Saxton's and Norden's pioneer work, produced his *Theatre of the Empire of Great Britaine*, adding excellent town plans, battle scenes, and magnificent coats of arms. The next great English map-maker was John Ogilby and, in 1675, he published *Britannia*, Volume I, in which all the roads of England and Wales were engraved on a scale of one inch to the mile, in a massive series of strip maps. From this time onwards, no map was published without roads, and, throughout the eighteenth century, steady progress was made in accuracy, if not always in the beauty of presentation.

The first Ordnance Survey maps came about as a result of Bonnie Prince Charlie's Jacobite rebellion of 1745. It was, however, in 1791, following the successful completion of the military survey of Scotland by General Roy that the Ordnance Survey was formally established. The threat of invasion by Napoleon in the early nineteenth century spurred on the demand for accurate and detailed mapping for military purposes, and, to meet this need, the first Ordnance Survey one-inch map, covering part of Essex, was published in 1805 in a single colour. This was the first numbered sheet in the First Series of one-inch maps.

Over the next seventy years, the one-inch map was extended to cover the whole of Great Britain. Reprints of some of the First Series maps, incorporating various later nineteenth-century amendments, have been published by David & Charles. The reprinted sheets covering most of our area are Numbers 12, 13, 16, and 17.

The Ordnance Survey's one-inch maps evolved through a number of 'Series' and 'Editions' to the Seventh Series which was replaced in 1974 by the metric 1:50 000 scale Landranger Series. Between the First Series one-inch and the current Landranger maps, many changes in style, format, content, and purpose have taken place. Colour, for example, first appeared with the timid use of light brown for hill shading on the 1889 one-inch sheets. By 1892, as many as five colours were being used for this scale and, at one stage, the Seventh Series was being printed in no less than ten colours. Recent developments in 'process printing' — a technique in which four basic colours produce any required tint — are now used to produce Ordnance Survey Landranger and other maps series. Through the years, the one-inch Series has gradually turned away from its military origins and has developed to meet a wider user demand. The modern, detailed, full-colour Landranger maps at 1:50 000 scale incorporate Rights of Way and Tourist Information, and are much used for both leisure and business purposes. To compare the old and new approaches to changing demand, see the two map extracts of Dartmouth on the following pages.

Modern Ordnance Survey Maps of the Area

South Devon and Dartmoor are covered by Ordnance Survey 1:50 000 scale (11/4 inches to 1 mile) Landranger map sheets 180, 181, 190, 191, 192, 193, 201 and 202. These all-purpose maps are ideal to help you explore the area. Viewpoints, picnic sites, places of interest, caravan and camping sites are shown, as well as public rights of way information such as footpaths and bridleways.

Dartmoor is also covered by a single map in the Ordnance Survey Touring Map series at a scale of 1 inch to 1 mile.

The walker is well catered for by two Ordnance Survey 1:25 000 scale (21/2 inches to 1 mile) Outdoor Leisure Maps:

Sheet 20 — South Devon
Sheet 28 — Dartmoor

The areas surrounding these two sheets are also covered at 1:25 000 scale for the walker by the Ordnance Survey Pathfinder series

Motorists will find the Ordnance Survey 1:250 000 scale (1 inch to 4 miles) Routemaster map most useful:

Sheet 8 — South West England and South Wales

An alternative will be found in the form of the Ordnance Survey Motoring Atlas of Great Britain at the larger scale of 1 inch to 3 miles.

To place the area in historical context, the following in the Historical Map and Guide series will be of use: Ancient Britain, Roman Britain, and Britain before the Norman Conquest.

The above maps, and other Ordnance Survey products, are available from most booksellers, stationers and newsagents, or the approved Ordnance Survey stockists below:

Eland Bros.
22 Bedford Street
Exeter, EX1 1LE
Tel 0392 55788

Kenroy Thompson Limited
25 Cobourg Street
Plymouth, PL1 1SR
Tel 0752 227693

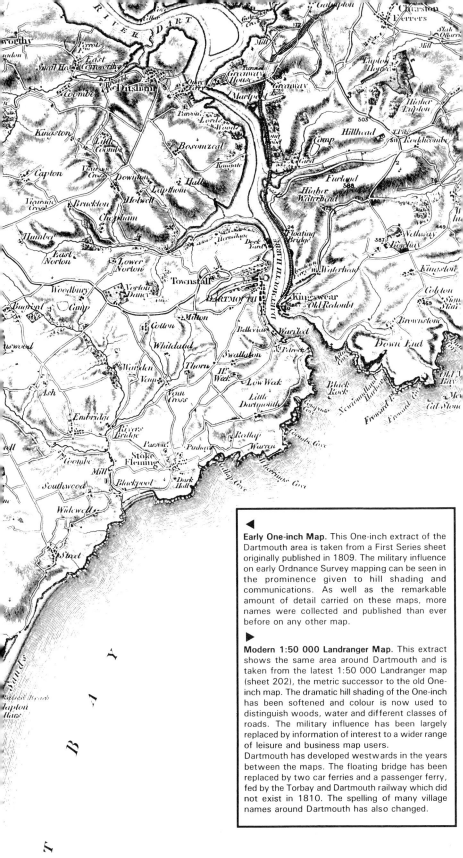

▲

Early One-inch Map. This One-inch extract of the Dartmouth area is taken from a First Series sheet originally published in 1809. The military influence on early Ordnance Survey mapping can be seen in the prominence given to hill shading and communications. As well as the remarkable amount of detail carried on these maps, more names were collected and published than ever before on any other map.

▶

Modern 1:50 000 Landranger Map. This extract shows the same area around Dartmouth and is taken from the latest 1:50 000 Landranger map (sheet 202), the metric successor to the old One-inch map. The dramatic hill shading of the One-inch has been softened and colour is now used to distinguish woods, water and different classes of roads. The military influence has been largely replaced by information of interest to a wider range of leisure and business map users.

Dartmouth has developed westwards in the years between the maps. The floating bridge has been replaced by two car ferries and a passenger ferry, fed by the Torbay and Dartmouth railway which did not exist in 1810. The spelling of many village names around Dartmouth has also changed.

Index

Selected further reading

Bidwell, Paul. *Roman Exeter: Fortress and Town*. 1980. Exeter City Council.

British Geological Survey. *British Regional Geology: South-west England*. 1975. HMSO.

Byng, Brian. *Dartmoor's Mysterious Megaliths*. Baron Jay Ltd.

Crossing, W; Le Messurier, Brian (ed.) *Guide to Dartmoor*. 1965. David & Charles.

Forrester, R A. *What was an Atmospheric Railway?* 1987.

Gant, Tom. *Discover Dartmoor*. 1978. Baron Jay Ltd.

Harris, Helen. *The Industrial Archaeology of Dartmoor*. 1978. David & Charles.

Hoskins, W G. *Devon*. 1972. David & Charles.

Le Messurier, Brian. *The Visitor's Guide to Devon*. 1988. Moorland Publishing.

Morgan, Martyn. *Becky Falls Spotter Guide*. 1987.

Pike, John. *Magic Town: A Portrait of Torbay*. 1988. Torbay Borough Council.

Redhead, Brian. *The National Parks of England and Wales*. 1989. Oxford Illustrated Press.

Room, Adrian. *Pocket Guide to British Place Names*. 1985. Longman

Tavy, Peter. *Walk Dartmoor*. 1984. Bartholomew.

Weir, John (ed.).*Dartmoor National Park*. 1987. Webb & Bower.